SUNSTROKE

Sunstroke

Selected Stories of
Ivan Bunin

TRANSLATED FROM THE RUSSIAN
AND WITH AN INTRODUCTION BY
GRAHAM HETTLINGER

Ivan R. Dee
CHICAGO 2002

Grateful acknowledgment is made to the *Hudson Review*, where a slightly different version of "Rusya" first appeared, and to the *Kenyon Review*, where slightly different versions of "Raven" and "Caucasus" first appeared.

Library of Congress Cataloging-in-Publication Data:
Bunin, Ivan Alekseevich, 1870–1953.
    [Short stories. English. Selections]
    Sunstroke : selected stories of Ivan Bunin / translated from the Russian, with an introduction by Graham Hettlinger.
    p. cm.
    Includes bibliographical references.
    ISBN 1-56663-426-1 (alk. paper)
    1. Bunin, Ivan Alekseevich, 1870–1953—Translations into English.
I. Hettlinger, Graham. II. Title.

PG3453.B9 A24 2002
891.73'3—dc21   2001052563

For Mila, who made this possible

Contents

Acknowledgments

DANIEL COLLINS, Irene Masing Delic, Terrence Graham, Karen Hettlinger, Mary Hettlinger, Jared Ingersoll, Maria Lekic, and Holly Stephens provided helpful comments and suggestions on these translations. I am particularly indebted to Angela Brintlinger for her comments on earlier drafts of many of these works, and to Richard Davis for his encouragement and his teaching on the art of translation.

Finally, I would like to thank my wife, Mila Medina. The many hours she devoted to the review and correction of these translations, her sensitivity to the subtleties of the Russian language, and her insightful knowledge of the author were vital to the completion of this work.

G. H.

Bethesda, Maryland
January 2002

Introduction

IVAN BUNIN (1870–1953) is as widely known in Russia today as any of the great nineteenth-century realists with whom he is often associated, including his idol, Leo Tolstoy, and his friend, Anton Chekhov. Virtually every educated Russian reader is familiar with such works as "Ida" (1925), "Sunstroke" (1925), *The Life of Arsenyev* (1927–1928), and *Dark Avenues* (1946). Scores of critical studies of his poetry and prose have been published since the 1960s, and new editions of his writings have continued to disappear quickly from Russian bookstores during the past twenty years.[1]

Bunin did not live to see this lasting recognition of his work.

---

1. A. Tvardovsky, "O Bunine," in I. A. Bunin, *Sobraniye Sochineny v Shesti Tomakh* (Moskva: Khudozhestvennaya Literatura, 1987) v. 1, 6.

Already established as one of the country's most important authors, he fled Russia shortly after the 1917 Revolution, and his writings were soon banned. Under Stalin, the Soviet government launched a systematic campaign to destroy already existing volumes of his work, and in the 1940s it became a punishable offense even to mention the author by name.[2]

Bunin eventually settled in Grasse, France, where he entered a period of remarkable productivity, completing more than forty-five short stories between 1920 and 1930, and beginning his autobiographical novel, *The Life of Arsenyev*, in 1927. These works, combined with such celebrated masterpieces as "The Gentleman from San Francisco" (1915), gained him a dedicated following among Russian emigré writers and critics as well as several major European authors, including André Gide, Ranier Maria Rilke, and Thomas Mann.[3] In 1933, Bunin's acclaim reached its apogee when he became the first Russian writer to receive the Noble Prize for literature. But this renown proved temporary, and by the mid-1930s he was struggling to survive on meager royalties and nominal pay for public readings.

Having endured great deprivations during World War II and the German occupation of Grasse, Bunin published his last collection of short stories, *Dark Avenues*, in 1946. Critics today widely agree that this collection of passionate, often erotic love stories is one of Bunin's finest works, but it received virtually no serious critical attention when it first appeared in print,[4] and its frank treatment of human sexuality offended many of the au-

2. Yury Maltsev, *Bunin* (Frankfurt, Moscow: Possev-Verlag, 1987), 6.
3. A. K. Baboreko, "Poeziya i Pravda Bunina," in *Zhizn Bunina*, by V. N. Muromtseva-Bunina (Moskva: Sovetsky Pisatel, 1989), 19.
4. Robert Woodward, *Ivan Bunin: A Study of His Fiction* (Chapel Hill: University of North Carolina Press, 1980), 17.

thor's most loyal readers. The book's financial and critical failure was a heavy blow for Bunin. He was soon reduced to begging friends and supporters for money in order to survive until his death in Paris in 1953.[5]

Although his "rehabilitation" in the Soviet Union eventually led to Bunin's inclusion among the ranks of Russia's greatest writers, he has remained largely unknown to English-language readers. Even his most famous story, "The Gentleman from San Francisco," which Thomas Mann considered a masterpiece equal to Tolstoy's *Death of Ivan Ilych*,[6] is rarely read in the United States. Both "Ida" and "In Paris" (1940), two of Bunin's finest works, have not been translated into English in more than fifty years, and seven of the stories included in this volume— "Summer Day" (1930), "First Class" (1930), "Old Woman" (1930), "Sky Above a Wall" (1930), "Old and Young" (1936), and "Ballad" (1938)—appear in English for the first time. To date, no complete translation of *Dark Avenues* has been published in English; thirteen of the stories in this collection are taken from that volume.

Bunin began his literary career as a poet, and it was his verse that first gained him widespread recognition in Russia before the Revolution. Although he stopped publishing poetry in the mid-1920s, Bunin continued to refer to himself as a poet throughout his life, and he stated repeatedly that his prose was born from his verse. "What torture it is to find the sound, the melody of a story—that sound which determines everything that follows," he once complained. "Until I find that sound, I cannot write."[7]

5. Julian Connolly, *Ivan Bunin* (Boston: G. K. Hall, 1982), 16.
6. Anna Saakyants, notes to "Gospodin iz San-Frantsisko," in I. A. Bunin, *Sochineniya v Trekh Tomakh* (Moskva: Khudozhestvennaya Literatura, 1982) v. 2, 535.
7. Ibid., 534.

The lyric impulse that motivated so much of Bunin's writing is evident throughout the stories collected here. In the prose miniatures, such as "Summer Day" and "Sky Above a Wall," he seeks only to capture a momentary impression or a passing scene rather than writing a traditional narrative. And even in his longer works, Bunin displays little interest in exploring the psychology of his characters or creating detailed plots. Instead these stories are primarily shaped by an urge to express both the intense, sensual pleasure of existence and the tragic fleetingness of life. Thus, even as they depict a wide range of passionate affairs, seductions, betrayals, and deaths, they tend to read more like poetry than potboilers, delivering their most powerful effects through the rhythms and pacing of their sentences, their highly detailed, sensuous imagery, and the connotative richness of their language.

The great importance of poetry in Bunin's prose makes it impossible to translate his work in its true entirety. One must constantly choose between a "literal" rendition of the original word or a rough equivalent that might preserve the rhythmic qualities and rich connotations of the Russian. Regardless, something is inevitably lost. And English is particularly inhospitable to Bunin's style. The inflected structure of the Russian language allows for enormously pliant syntax, which Bunin uses for maximum effect. He loves to insert a long descriptive phrase between a verb and its object, for example, in order to suspend a moment in time, or to surround a noun with complex modifiers so that an object slowly comes into increasingly sharp focus as the reader moves through the sentence. But its strict rules of word order make English far more rigid than Russian. Modifiers must be neatly saddled on their nouns; too much intervening detail between a verb and its object quickly results in confusion. Thus a sentence that unfolds with luxuriant ease in Russian can quickly turn prolix and ungainly in English.

In the translations that follow, I have attempted to preserve some of the fluidity, the precision, and the rhythms of Bunin's original prose. As part of that effort, I have allowed myself to break up and rearrange sentences in order to create linguistic effects in English that resemble those of the original, even if the form producing these effects is quite unlike the Russian form. When a literal translation of a Russian phrase would have resulted in a tired, English cliché—a cliché that did not mar the original—I have attempted to find a close alternative that remains true to the spirit of the Russian. In instances where the repeated use of multiple modifiers would transform a richly textured Russian sentence into something overwrought and amateurish in English, I have tried to use one adjective that could adequately substitute for two in the original. This means, of course, that readers will not find an exact replica of Bunin's prose in the following pages. I hope, however, that they will encounter some slight echo of its music and its grace.

SUNSTROKE

Sunstroke

T HEY CAME from the hot, brightly lit dining room onto the ship's deck after dinner and stood by the handrail. She closed her eyes, pressed the back of her hand against her cheek, and laughed. Her laughter was simple and pleasant, as was everything about this small, attractive woman.

"I think I'm drunk," she said. "Where did you come from? Three hours ago I didn't even know you existed. I don't even know where you got on this boat. Samara? Well, I guess it doesn't matter. . . . Is my head spinning, or are we turning?"

Darkness and distant lights hung before them. But now the lights fell away; a strong, soft breeze rose from the darkness and blew into their faces as the steamer veered to one side — describing an expansive, slightly grandiose arc, it seemed to flaunt the Volga's breadth — and then approached a small pier.

The lieutenant brought her hand to his lips: small and tan, it smelled of the sun. He imagined that all the skin beneath her gingham dress was equally as strong and tan, for she had said that she was coming from Anapa, where she'd spent a solid month lying under the hot southern sun on the sand by the sea—and this thought made his heart go still with fear and joy.

"Let's get off," he mumbled.

"Where?" she asked, surprised.

"On that pier."

"Why?"

He didn't answer. She lay the back of her hand against her warm cheek again.

"Insanity. . . ."

"Let's get off," the lieutenant repeated stupidly. "I'm begging you."

"Oh, all right. As you wish . . . ," she said, turning away.

They almost fell over each other when the steamer bumped with a soft thud against the dimly lit pier. A mooring line flew over their heads; the water seemed to boil as the engines reversed and pushed the ship back toward the dock, and then the gangplanks dropped with a bang—the lieutenant rushed to get their bags.

A moment later they emerged from a drowsy little office on the dock, crossed a patch of ankle-deep sand, and climbed into a dusty cab without exchanging words. Soft with dust and lit by only a few crooked lamps, the road seemed endless as they traveled its gradual slope up the mountainside. But at last they reached the top and began to rattle down a paved carriageway past little offices, the local watchtower, a public square. It was warm, and the air was heavy with all the smells of a provincial town on a summer night. The driver stopped before the lighted entrance to an inn, the open doors of which displayed a worn, steep wooden staircase. An old, unshaven porter with big, wide feet, a pink shirt, and a frock coat sullenly took their bags and lugged them up the steps. They entered a large room that was terribly stuffy and still sweltering from the day's sun; white curtains were closed over the windows and two unused candles stood on the mantelpiece. As soon as the porter left and shut the door, the lieutenant rushed to her with such ardent desire, and they both gasped with such ecstasy as they kissed, that each would remember that moment for many years to come: they had never experienced anything similar in all their separate lives.

The next morning was cheerful, sunny, and hot, and at ten o'clock—while church bells rang, while people shopped at a market near the inn, while the warm air was filled with the smell of hay and tar and all the other complex, pungent odors of a provincial Russian town—that small, anonymous woman, who refused to say her name and jokingly referred to herself as "the beautiful stranger," went away. They had slept very little, but after washing and dressing for five minutes, she looked as fresh as a seventeen-year-old girl when she came out from behind the screen near the bed. Was she awkward or ashamed? Not very, no. Instead she was as happy and as open as she'd been the day before, and her mind was clear.

"No, no, darling," she'd said in answer to his request that they continue traveling together. "You should stay here and wait for the next boat. If we go together, everything will be ruined. It would be very unpleasant for me. I give you my honest word that I'm nothing like the person you might imagine me to be. Nothing even remotely similar to this has ever happened to me—and it never will again. I must have lost my mind. Or we've both suffered some kind of sunstroke."

For some reason the lieutenant easily agreed, and he rode with her to the pier in a lighthearted mood. They arrived just before the pink steamer *Samolyot* left the dock, and he kissed her openly on deck, despite the crowd, then jumped back onto the gangplank as it was being pulled away.

He returned to the inn feeling equally happy and carefree. But something had changed. The room seemed completely different from the room where she had been. It was still full of her, and yet, it was completely empty. How strange! The air still smelled of her English perfume, the cup from which she'd drunk her tea still stood half empty on the tray—and already she was gone. Overwhelmed by a sudden wave of tenderness and longing, the lieutenant hurriedly lit a cigarette and began to pace the room.

"What a strange adventure," he said out loud, laughing as he felt tears well up in his eyes. *I give you my honest word that I'm nothing like the person you might imagine me to be.* And then she's gone.

The screen had been moved aside; he put it back before the unmade bed, knowing that he couldn't bear to look at those sheets and pillows now. He shut the windows in order to escape the sound of carriage wheels creaking in the street and voices rising from the market, then he closed the filmy white curtains and sat down on the couch. Yes, this is it—the end of the "traveler's adventure." She's already gone, already far away, riding in a ship's salon that's all windows and white paint, or sitting on the deck, looking at the huge, gleaming surface of the river in the sun, looking at the yellow sandbars and the rafts drifting downstream, looking at the endless open space of the Volga and a horizon where shimmering water meets the sky. . . . Goodbye—say goodbye and that's it, always and forever. . . . For where could they possibly meet again? "I could never turn up in the town where she leads a normal life, has a husband and a three-year-old daughter, all her family," he thought to himself. Indeed, that town seemed to be an utterly forbidden place, and the thought that she would live out her lonely life there, often, perhaps, remembering their fleeting, chance encounter, while he would never see her again—this thought stunned him like a sharp, sudden blow. No, it couldn't be! It was too cruel, impossible, insane. The prospect of his life—all the painful, senseless years he'd spend without her—plunged him into horror and despair. "For God's sake!" he thought, struggling to keep his eyes from the bed behind the screen as he began to pace the room again. "What's wrong with me? What is it about her? What exactly happened yesterday? It must be some kind of sunstroke! And now I'm stuck in this backwater without her. How the hell will I get through the day?"

He still remembered everything about her, remembered all the small, fine details of her presence—the smell of her suntanned skin and her gingham dress, her supple body, the simple, uplifting sound of her voice. Traces of the exquisite pleasure that she'd given him with all her feminine charm remained extraordinarily acute within him, but those sensations were now eclipsed by a strange new feeling that he couldn't comprehend. He could never have imagined such a feeling taking hold of him when he pursued her yesterday, seeking what he thought would be a casual acquaintance; when they were together, there'd been no hint of it—and now it was impossible to tell her what he felt! "I'll never have the chance," he thought. "That's the worst of all—I'll never get to speak to her again! And what now? . . . Memories I can't dispel. . . . Pain I can't relieve. . . . An interminable day stuck in this godforsaken town. And the Volga shining in the sun while it carries her away on a pink steamer!"

He had to save himself somehow—occupy his mind with something, go somewhere, find some kind of diversion. He put his hat on decisively, picked up his riding crop, and quickly passed through the empty corridor, his spurs chinking. "But where am I going?" he wondered as he bolted down the steep wooden stairs. A young driver waited near the hotel entrance, wearing a trim, sleeveless coat and placidly smoking a cigarette. The lieutenant looked at him uncomprehendingly. "How can he just sit there on his coach, smoke a cigarette, and be perfectly content, carefree, resigned? I must be the only person in this town who feels so miserable," he thought, heading toward the market.

The market was closing down, and many of the merchants had already driven off. But for some reason he walked among the fresh droppings left by the horses, walked among the wagons and carts loaded with cucumbers, the displays of new pots and bowls. And all of it—the men who overwhelmed him with their shouts of *Here's a first class cucumber, your lordship,* and the women sitting on the ground who vied for his attention, urging him to come closer as they lifted up their pots and rapped them with their knuckles to prove they had no cracks—all of it seemed so stupid and absurd that he quickly ran away and went inside a church, where the choristers were singing with emphatic joy and confidence, and a keen awareness of the duty they were carrying out. Then he wandered into a small, neglected garden on the mountain's edge and slowly walked around in circles, the river's measureless expanse shining like bright steel beneath him. . . .

The shoulder straps and buttons of his uniform grew too hot to touch. The inside of his cap turned wet with sweat. His face began to burn. . . . When he returned to the inn he felt a certain pleasure as he entered the spacious, cool, and empty dining room on the lower floor. He felt pleasure as he removed his hat and sat down at a small table by an open window that let a little air into the room despite the heat. He ordered *botvinya* with ice. . . . Everything was good. There was enormous happiness in everything. Even the heat; even the smells of the marketplace and this unfamiliar, little town; even this old, provincial inn contained great joy: and in its midst his heart was being torn to shreds. . . . He ate half-sour pickles with dill and downed four shots of vodka, thinking he'd die willingly tomorrow if some miracle would let him bring her back, let him spend one more day with her just so he could tell her everything. That was all he wanted now—to convince her, to show her how ecstatically and miserably he loved her. . . . What for? Why try to convince her? Why show her anything? He didn't know, but this was more essential than his life.

"I'm falling completely apart," he said out loud, and poured another drink.

He pushed his bowl of soup away, ordered black coffee, and began to smoke, wondering desperately what he could do to save himself from this sudden, completely unexpected love. But even as he sought some means of escape, he felt all too clearly that escaping was impossible. And suddenly he got up again, grabbed his hat and riding crop, asked directions to the post office, and hurried off—a telegram already written in his head: "My entire life is yours from this day on—completely yours, forever, until I die." But he stopped in horror as he approached the old, squat building that housed the postal center: he knew the town where she lived, knew she had a husband and a three-year-old daughter, but he didn't know her name! He'd asked her several times at dinner and at the hotel, but she had only laughed. *Why do you need to know my name, or who I am?*

A shop window on the corner near the post office was filled with photographs. He looked for a long time at the portrait of some military type with bulging eyes, a low forehead, and a stunning pair of lavish sideburns. He wore thick epaulets, and his exceedingly broad chest was completely covered with medals. . . . How terrible and savage everything mundane and ordinary becomes when the heart's been destroyed—yes, he understood that now—destroyed by sunstroke, destroyed by too much happiness and love. He glanced at a photograph of two newlyweds—a young man with a crew cut stood at attention in a long frock coat and a white tie, his bride in a gauzy wedding dress on his arm— then moved his eyes to the portrait of an attractive, upper-class girl with an ardent expression and a student's cap cocked to one side on her head. And then, overwhelmed with envy for all these unknown people who were free of suffering, he began to study the street, looking desperately for something.

Where to? What now?

The street was completely empty and all the buildings looked identical: white, two-story merchant-class homes with big gardens and not a soul inside. A thick white dust lay on the paving stones; and all of it was blinding, all of it was flooded with hot, joyful, flaming sunlight which now seemed useless beyond words. The street rose in the distance, then dipped down, as if stooping under the cloudless sky. The glare reflected from its surface turned the horizon slightly grey, which reminded him of the south of Sevastopol, Kerch, Anapa. And that was more than he could bear: stumbling and tripping on his spurs, squinting in the light, struggling to see the ground beneath his feet, the lieutenant staggered back the way he'd come.

When he reached the inn, he was as exhausted as a man who'd marched for miles in Turkestan or the Sahara. Gathering the last of his strength, he re-entered his large and empty room: it had been cleaned—every trace of her was gone except for a forgotten hairpin that now lay on the nightstand. He removed his jacket and glanced at his reflection in the mirror: his moustache had been bleached white and his face looked grey from the sun; the whites of his eyes—slightly tinged with blue—stood out sharply against his darkened skin. It was an ordinary officer's face, but it now looked haggard and deranged, and there was something both youthful and profoundly sad about his thin white shirt and its small starched collar. He lay down on his back on the bed and propped his dusty boots up on the footboard. The curtains hung loose before the open windows, rustling occasionally as a small breeze blew into the room, laden with more heat from the scorching metal roofs—more heat from all the silent, glaring, lifeless world around him. He put his hands behind his head and stared fixedly in front of him, then clenched his teeth and closed his eyes, feeling tears spill down his cheeks—and finally, he dozed off. It was evening when he awoke: a red and yellow sun hung behind the curtains, the breeze had died away, the room felt as hot and dry as an oven. When the morning and the day before resurfaced in his memory, it seemed they'd taken place ten years ago.

He rose unhurriedly and washed, opened the curtains, asked for his bill and a samovar, slowly drank a cup of tea with lemon. Then he ordered a driver, had his bags brought out, climbed into the coach's rusty, sun-scorched seat, and handed five whole rubles to the porter.

"I think it was me who brought you here last night," the driver said cheerfully, picking up his reins.

The summer evening sky had already turned dark blue above the Volga by the time they reached the dock. Different colored lights were scattered in profusion along the river; other, larger lights hung in the masts of an approaching steamer.

"Right on time," the driver said ingratiatingly.

The lieutenant tipped him five rubles as well, bought his ticket, walked out onto the landing. Everything was like the day before: a soft blow to the pier and a slight giddiness as it rocks underfoot, a glimpse of the mooring line flying through the air; and then the engine's thrown into reverse, the river surges forward from the paddle wheel, and the water seems to boil as the steamer's driven back toward the dock. . . . This time the ship seemed unusually welcoming: its brightly lit deck was crowded with people, and the air smelled of cooking smoke from the galley.

A moment later they were being carried up the river, just as she'd been carried off so recently.

The summer dusk was dying out in the distance ahead: it glowed in drowsy, muted colors on the water, while trembling ripples flashed sporadically beneath the last, spent traces of the setting sun—and all the lights scattered in the surrounding dark kept on drifting, drifting off.

The lieutenant sat under an awning on deck, feeling like he'd aged ten years.

[1925]

Summer Day

A SETTLEMENT on the outskirts of Russia. An endless summer day.

And all day a bootmaker sitting barefoot on a rotting bench near a tumbledown shack, his belt unbuckled and his long shirt hanging loose, the sun beating down on his shaggy head. He sits there killing time with a red dog.

"Shake!"

The dog doesn't know the command.

"I said 'shake!'"

Still the dog doesn't offer his paw. The bootmaker slaps his muzzle. The dog bats his eyes in shock and disgust, turns away, bares his teeth—a bittersweet smile. Then he lifts one paw un-

certainly, drops it back to the ground. Another blow to the face.
And again—

"I told you to shake, you son of a bitch!"

[1930]

Raven

MY FATHER looked like a raven. This dawned on me when I was still a boy. I was looking at a picture in *Niva* of Napoleon standing on a cliff. He wore buckskin pants and short black boots, and his belly protruded slightly under his white shirt. Remembering another picture from *Bogdanov's Polar Expeditions*, I laughed out loud with joy: Napoleon looked like a penguin! And then I thought sadly, but father looks like a raven.

My father held a very prominent position in the government of our provincial town, and this ruined him even more. I think no one in the society of bureaucrats to which he belonged was so taciturn, gloomy, and severe. None of them spoke so slowly and so cruelly, or acted with such cold reserve. Round-shouldered, short, thick-set—with his coarse black hair, his prominent nose, and his long, dark, clean-shaven face he looked exactly like a raven. The similarity was particularly striking when he wore a black tuxedo with tails to the charity balls sponsored by the governor's wife. Stooping beside a refreshment stand that had been decorated to resemble a little peasant hut, he would raise his big raven head to study the room, glance with his shiny raven eyes at the dancers, at the people coming to the hut for drinks, and at the boyar's wife who would smile so charmingly as she served shallow glasses of cheap, yellow champagne—a sturdy woman wearing a brocade gown and a beaded, glittering head-dress, her big hands heavy with jewels, her nose so pink and white with powder that it no longer resembled human flesh. My father had been a widower for a long time; my eight-year-old sister Lilya and I were his only children. The second-story apartment that the government provided us looked out on a boulevard of poplars between the cathedral and the main street, and all the huge, empty rooms had a cold, mirrorlike sheen. Fortunately I spent more than half the year studying at the Katkovsky Lyceum in Moscow, returning home only for Christmas and summer vacation. That year, however, I came back to something completely unexpected. . . .

In the spring I had graduated from the lyceum, and when I returned from Moscow I was simply amazed: Lilya's nanny, a tall, skinny old woman who looked like a wooden statue of some medieval saint, had been replaced by a young, graceful girl, and her presence had transformed the house: it was as if the sun had suddenly begun to shine in those rooms that were once so life-less. The daughter of a poorly paid petty bureaucrat who served under my father, she was thrilled to have found good work immediately after graduating from high school, and when I arrived she was equally happy to have someone her own age in the household. But she was so cowed by my father that she trembled in his presence at our formal dinners while anxiously watching Lilya—an imperious little girl with black hair and black eyes, she was no less taciturn than our father, and she constantly turned her head from side to side as if waiting for something at the table, her silence as edgy as her movements. My father had become completely unrecognizable at these dinners. He no longer stared disapprovingly at old Gury as he served him with his hands in knitted gloves—instead he talked constantly, slowly enunciating his words and addressing only the new nanny. He called her ceremoniously by name and patronymic—"My dear Yelena Nikolayevna"—and even laughed and tried to joke. She was completely flustered by this display and responded only with a piteous smile—the smile of a thin, light-skinned girl whose delicate cheeks have begun to flush as sweat darkens the underarms of her white blouse, beneath which her breasts are barely noticeable. She never dared to look at me during those dinners: for her I was even more terrifying than my father. But the more she sought to avoid glancing at me, the more coldly my father looked in my direction: he and I both knew—sensed somehow—that she tried so painfully to hear only him and to serve only my ill-tempered, restless, and silent sister because she wanted desperately to hide another fear—a fear of the joy she and I felt in each other's presence. My father had always ordered tea in his study; he would drink it from a large cup edged in gold while working at his desk. But now he began to leave his study when Lilya was asleep and Yelena was free to sit at the samovar. Wearing a long, wide, double-breasted jacket with a red lining, he would appear in the dining room, settle into his armchair, and give his cup to her. She would fill it to the brim, just the way he liked, pass it back with trembling hands, and then, after filling a cup for me and for herself, she would lower her eyes and take up her embroidery while he launched into another slow, strange monologue:

"Dear Yelena Nikolayevna, I think fair-haired women like you look best in black or crimson. . . . A black satin dress with a stand-up, jagged collar a la Mary Stuart—one with little diamond studs—would look perfect on you. . . . Or a velvet, crimson dress in the medieval style—slightly *décolleté*, with a little ruby cross. . . . And a dark blue velvet coat with one of those Venetian berets—that would look splendid as well! But of course, that is all idle fantasy," he said, laughing. "Your father earns seventy-five rubles a month at our office, and he has five children in addition to you—'each one younger than the last'—and you, most likely, will be forced to live your entire life in poverty. But I will say this: what harm do dreams do? They enliven us, give us hope and strength. And does it really never happen that a dream comes true? Rarely, of course, very rarely—but sometimes, suddenly, a dream is brought to life. . . . Just recently, for instance, a simple cook at Kursk station won 200,000 rubles with a lottery ticket—a mere cook!"

She would force herself to look at him and smile, as if she understood these words to be a harmless joke, while I played Patience and pretended not to hear. Once he went even farther and nodded in my direction:

"And this young man—he too, of course, has dreams. 'One day,' he thinks, 'one day father will die, and then even my hens will grow tired of gold!' But he's quite mistaken. Papa does own a few things—an estate and several thousand acres of black soil in the Samara province, for instance, but there's little chance the boy will get his hands on that, for he has favored his father with decidedly little affection, and I see that he would make a first-class profligate. . . ."

That conversation took place just before Saint Peter's day—
I remember it well. The next morning my father left for church,
and from there he went to a luncheon in honor of the governor's
name day. He was never home for weekday lunches anyway, so
the three of us ate alone as usual. At the end of the meal, when
Lilya was given cherry *blancmange* instead of her favorite pas-
tries, she began to screech at Gury and pound her fists on the
table. Shaking her head hysterically, she threw her plate on the
floor and began choking with violent sobs. Somehow we man-
aged to drag her to her room, begging her to calm down and
promising to punish the cook severely while she kicked and bit at
our hands. Eventually she grew quiet and fell asleep—but what
fleeting tenderness Yelena and I had shared in that struggle!
Again and again our hands had lightly touched as we carried
Lilya away. The streets outside began to hiss with rain, lightning
flashed in the darkening rooms, and thunder rattled the windowpanes. "It's the thunderstorm that made her act that way," she
said joyfully when we went into the corridor; then she froze and
listened apprehensively. "There's a fire!"

We ran into the dining room and threw open a window—a
fire crew was roaring along the boulevard as the downpour
streamed through the poplars; the lightning had already stopped,
as if extinguished by the heavy rain. A bugler was sounding a
warning as men in copper helmets rumbled past on long carts
filled with ladders and hoses, and the notes he played seemed
almost lighthearted, almost tender and mischievous amid the
rattling wheels, the clattering hooves on the cobblestones, and
the jingling harness bells that shook above the horses' black
manes. . . . Then the city alarm rang out—again and again it
clanged from the bell tower of the Warrior Ivan. . . . We were
standing close to one another at the window; the fresh air

smelled of water and damp dust, and it seemed we were only listening, only looking with excitement at the street. Hauling big red tanks, the last of the carts flashed by, and with my heart beating hard, with my forehead tightening from fear, I took the hand that she held limply by her side and stared imploringly at her cheek. She turned pale, parted her lips, and sighed so deeply that her chest rose. Her eyes were full of tears, as if she too were pleading. I caught her by the shoulder, and then, for the first time in my life, I tasted the tender, intoxicating cold of a young girl's lips. . . . From that point on, not a day passed without our meeting, as if by accident, in the parlor, the living room, or the corridor, sometimes even in my father's study before he came home in the evening. And each meeting was always too short; each forbidden, despairing, drawn-out kiss only made us long for more. . . . As if sensing something, my father soon stopped coming to tea and grew silent and gloomy again. But we paid him no attention; even at dinner she seemed calm and more composed.

Early in July, Lilya gorged herself on raspberries and wound up sick. She spent hours drawing in her room as she slowly recovered, coloring imaginary cities with bright pastels on a sheet of paper tacked to a board. Yelena spent every day embroidering a blouse while she sat by Lilya's bed. It was impossible for her to leave the room—with every minute, Lilya had a new demand. Left alone in that empty, silent house, I felt as if I were dying from the constant desire to see Yelena, to kiss and embrace her again. I passed the time by sitting at my father's desk, opening the first book I pulled off his shelf, and forcing myself to read. And then one evening I heard her light, quick steps approaching the study. I jumped to my feet as she entered.

"What happened? Is she asleep?"

She waved her hand. "Oh no—of course not. You have no

idea—she can go for forty-eight hours without sleep and feel perfectly fine—like all lunatics! She has sent me here to find yellow
and orange pastels. . . ."

Beginning to cry, she came closer and rested her head on
my chest.

"My God, when will this end? Tell him once and for all that
you love me, that nothing can separate us!"

She raised her tear-streaked face and suddenly embraced
me, began to kiss me breathlessly. I pulled her body against mine
and moved toward the couch—how, in such a moment, could I
have thought more clearly? But suddenly I heard a cough, and,
looking across her shoulder, I saw my father in the doorway. He
stood and stared at us, then slouched away.

No one went to dinner. In the evening, Gury knocked on
my door. "Your father wishes to see you." I went into the study
and found him sitting at his desk. He began to speak without
turning to see me:

"Tomorrow you leave for my estate in Samara. You will
spend the summer there. In the autumn you will go to either
Moscow or Saint Petersburg to apply for a position in the government. If you dare to disobey me, I will completely disown you
forever. Furthermore, I am fully prepared to request that the governor send you to Samara under police escort if necessary. Now
get out of my sight and don't let me see you again. You will receive money for your trip and your living expenses in the morning from the servant. In the fall I will tell my estate manager to
provide for your move to the city. Do not even think of trying to
see her before you leave. That's all, dear child. Be off."

That night I left for the Yaroslavl province, where a friend of
mine from the lyceum lived. I stayed there until the fall. Then,
under his father's patronage, I moved to Saint Petersburg, en-

tered the ministry of foreign affairs, and wrote to my father, formally renouncing my inheritance and all other assistance from him. In the winter I learned that he had retired and moved to Saint Petersburg with, as I was told, "a charming little wife." And so it happened that I saw them one evening when I entered the Mariinsky Theatre just before the curtain rose. They were sitting in a box near the stage; on the barrier before them lay a pair of opera glasses made from mother-of-pearl. He still resembled a raven as he hunched in his seat, wearing a tuxedo and squinting one eye to read the program, while she, holding herself with elegance and poise, looked excitedly at the murmuring crowd that filled the hall below her, the glittering light of the chandeliers, the tuxedos, evening gowns, and uniforms of people entering their private boxes. Her light hair was arranged in an elaborate bouffant, and her bare arms, although still delicate, looked slightly heavier. She wore a cloak of crimson velvet, and it was fastened over her left shoulder with a ruby pin; she wore a little ruby cross around her neck, and it glowed like a dark red flame.

[1944]

Sky Above a Wall

I'M LEAVING Rome on a sunny winter morning.

The old cabby driving me to the train station is excited and drunk. Dressed lightly in a jacket and a cap, he sits high on the coach box, his elbows jabbing the air as he drives his skinny nag at a hard run through the shadows and the fresh damp of the narrow streets. Suddenly the road turns sharply to the right and drops down to a large square, flooded by the warm, blinding sun. The horse's hind legs buckle beneath her, and the old man, falling to the side, pulls hard on the brake. The wheels scrape and whine, the nag's hooves clatter loudly on the stones. In the damp and brilliant light still wavering before us, a huge fountain throws out thick grey columns of water, its spray hanging in the air like dust and smoke, while a long, crude wall—some ancient ruin resembling a rampart—slides slowly past us on the left, its stones resplendent in the sun, its top bordered by the thick, bright azure of the sky. As he brakes, the old man lifts his eyes to that astounding and divine expanse of color, shouts, cries out: "Madonna! Madonna!"

[1930]

Ida

FOUR OF US — three old friends and a certain Georgy Ivanovich — had breakfast at the Bolshoy Moskovsky at Christmas time.

The restaurant was empty and cool on account of the holiday. We passed through the old hall, which was filled with a pale light from the icy, grey morning, and stopped at the entrance to the new dining room. The tables there had just been set with fresh, trim white cloths, and we looked them over carefully, wondering which would suit us best. Then the *maitre d'*, who was so well scrubbed and courteous he seemed to shine, made a refined and humble gesture toward a round booth in the corner. We followed his suggestion.

"Gentlemen," the composer said as he moved around the table and settled his solid frame firmly on the couch, "For some

reason I'd like to treat you all to a real feast today. Do you remember the magic tablecloth from all those fairy tales you read
as a child?" he said, turning his wide peasant face and narrow
eyes to the waiter. "We need a tablecloth like that. And a meal
even more generous than those it produced for the hungry
prince. You know my regal habits."

"Of course, Pavel Nikolayevich," answered the waiter, an
intelligent old man with a clean silver beard. "In fact, we've
learned your habits by heart," he said, smiling with restraint as he
placed an ashtray on the table. "Relax and enjoy yourself. We'll
do our best."

A moment later the table was set with champagne flutes,
goblets, and shot glasses, an assortment of flavored vodkas, pink
salmon, cracked oysters on ice, filets of smoked and salted stur-
geon, an orange block of Cheshire cheese, a black glistening
square of pressed caviar, and a frosted silver tub of champagne
bottles. . . . We started with the pepper vodka. . . . The composer
enjoyed filling our glasses himself. He poured three shots, then
paused:

"Most holy Georgy Ivanovich, may I indulge you?" he asked
jokingly.

A quiet, invariably good-humored man whose only occupation consisted of befriending well-known writers, artists, and
actors, Georgy Ivanovich blushed—as he always did—before
speaking.

"You certainly may, most sinful Pavel Nikolayevich," he said
with slightly excessive familiarity.

The composer poured him a drink, lightly touched glasses
with each of us, tossed back his vodka with the words "gracious
God," then exhaled through his moustache and set to work on
the hors d'oeuvres. The rest of us turned to the food as well; it

held our attention for quite a long time. Then we ordered *ukha* and paused in the meal to smoke. A sad, tender song began to play indistinctly on the phonograph in the old hall. The composer leaned back in his seat and drew on his cigarette. Then he raised his chest high and took a deep breath, as was his habit before speaking.

"Despite the pleasure my belly is enjoying, I'm sad today, friends," he said. "I'm sad because this morning, just as I was waking up, I remembered a trivial little story that took place exactly three years ago on the second day of Christmas. It involved a friend of mine who, in the course of events, was shown to be a complete ass."

"A trivial story, but no doubt an amorous one," said Georgy Ivanovich, with his girlish smile.

The composer cast a sidelong glance at him. "Amorous," he said sardonically. "Georgy Ivanovich—my dear Georgy Ivanovich, how will you ever answer for your salaciousness and your merciless wit on Judgment Day? May God be with you then. *"Je veux un trésor qui les contient tous, je veux la jeunesse"*— he raised his eyebrows as he sang along with the phonograph, which was playing Faust, and then continued to address us:

"Well, here is the story, friends. . . . Once upon a time, in an unknown land, a certain girl visited the home of a certain gentleman. A university friend of his wife's, she was so pleasant and unassuming that the gentleman referred to her simply by first name—Ida. Just Ida. He wasn't even completely sure of her patronymic or her last name. He knew that she came from a respectable but modest family, that she was the daughter of a musician who was once a well-known conductor, and that she lived with her parents while waiting, in the customary manner, for a groom to appear—and that was all.

"How can I describe this Ida to you? The gentleman was very well disposed toward her, but I repeat, he paid her no particular attention. She comes to the house and he says, 'Ah, Ida my dear, hello, hello. I'm very glad to see you.' She only smiles in response, hides her handkerchief inside her muff, and looks at him with the clear, slightly thoughtless eyes of a young girl. 'Is Masha here?' she asks. 'Of course, of course,' the gentleman answers, 'please come in.' 'Can I see her?' Ida asks, and casually walks through the dining room to Masha's door. 'Masha, can I come in?' Her voice rises from somewhere low in her chest. It's deep and velvety and it stirs him to his bones. Add to that voice all the vigor of youth and good health, the fresh scent of a girl entering a room from the cold. She's tall and slim, her figure's exquisite, and she moves with a rare, completely natural grace. Her face is particularly unusual: at first glance it seems completely ordinary, but look closely and you're lost. Her complexion is warm and even, like the slight blush of a fine apple. Her eyes are almost violet, bright, and full of life.

"Yes, look closely, and you're lost. And that ass—I mean, the hero of our story—he looks at her and goes into raptures: 'Ida, dear Ida,' he sighs. 'You don't know your own worth.' He sees her smiling as he says these words, and her expression is sweet but somehow slightly distracted. So the damn fool leaves—goes back to his study and occupies himself with some bit of nonsense that he calls a work of art.

"Time moved steadily along, and the gentleman never once thought seriously about this Ida until one fine day she disappeared. As you might imagine, he didn't notice in the least. Ida's gone. She's gone and he never thinks to ask his wife, 'Where has our friend Ida disappeared to?' Occasionally he feels something missing. He imagines the sweet anguish he would have suffered if he'd slipped his arms around her waist. He recalls the squirrel fur muff she carried, her English skirt, her delicate hands and pure complexion, her violet eyes. He remembers these things, feels a momentary pang of longing, and then forgets again. Two years went by that way.

"And then one day the hero of our story had to make a journey to the western regions of that mythical land in which he lived. It was Christmastime, but he had to go, regardless of the holiday. So he said farewell to his family and his subjects, rode off on his finest stallion. He rides all day and rides all night, until at last he reaches the regional station where he has a connection to make. But I should add that he arrives very late, and as soon as the train slows at the platform, he jumps off and grabs the first porter he sees by the collar. 'The express to so-and-so, has it left yet?' he shouts. The porter smiles politely. 'It just left, sir,' he says. 'You were pleased to arrive almost two hours late, after all, sir.' 'What?' The gentleman shouts. 'Are you joking? You fool! What am I supposed to do now! I'll send you to Siberia! To hard labor! I'll have you on the chopping block!' 'You are right, sir,' the porter answers. 'I'm obviously at fault. But as the saying goes, "those confessing sins are spared the sword." And there will be a local train, sir, that goes to that destination. Perhaps you'll be so good as to wait for it.' Our distinguished traveler bowed his head and plodded off to the station.

"It was pleasant and warm inside, crowded but comfortable. A blizzard had been blowing through the area for a full week, and the entire line was a mess—all the schedules had been shot to hell, and the transfer stations were jammed. Here it was just the same—people and luggage scattered everywhere, meals served at the counters all day, the smell of cooking smoke and samovar coals heavy in the air—all of which, as you know, is far from unpleasant in the midst of a blizzard and the freezing cold. Furthermore, this particular station was quite well appointed— clean and spacious—and the traveler realized right away that it would be no great tragedy to wait there, even for day. 'I'll clean myself up, then have a few drinks and a good meal,' he thought with pleasure as he entered the passengers' hall, and immediately set about completing his plan. The gentleman shaved, washed, put on a clean shirt, and fifteen minutes later he left the washroom looking twenty years younger. At the buffet he drank two shots, following the first with a *pirog* and the second with some Jewish pike. He was ready to order a third when suddenly, from somewhere behind him, he heard a female voice that was both terribly familiar and beautiful beyond words. He turned— 'with a pounding heart,' of course—and whom do you think he saw? Ida!

"At first he was so overwhelmed with astonishment and joy that he couldn't utter a word. He just stared at her like a sheep studying a new gate to its pasture. But she—and this, friends, is what it means to be a woman—she didn't bat an eye. Of course she couldn't help being somewhat surprised, and even a certain joy was evident in her expression, but all in all, I tell you, she stayed remarkably composed. 'My dear,' she says, 'what fates have produced this happy meeting!' Her eyes revealed that she meant what she was saying, but she spoke, somehow, too simply, and the tone of her words was nothing like it used to be. It had become, somehow, ironic, even slightly mocking. Our gentleman was amazed by the many other ways in which she'd changed as well. It was overwhelming—she'd bloomed like some kind of exotic flower kept in a crystalline vase with the cleanest water, and now she was virtually unrecognizable as she stood before him in a sable cloak worth a thousand rubles and a hellishly expensive winter hat, both of which combined pure modesty with sheer coquettishness. Dazzled by the rings on her fingers, he timidly kissed her hand, and Ida tipped back her head, said nonchalantly, 'By the way, please meet my husband': a student stepped out from behind her and neatly presented himself in military fashion."

"What insolence!" exclaimed Georgy Ivanovich, "An ordinary student!"

"But that's just it, dear Georgy Ivanovich," the composer said with a bitter smile. "There was nothing ordinary about him. In fact, our gentleman had never in his life seen such a striking example of what is called nobility as this young man, whose features were as white and smooth as marble. He wore a double-breasted jacket. It was sewn from that light, grey cloth that only the most stylish gentlemen wear, and it was tailored perfectly to his trim waist. The rest of his wardrobe was equally refined and elegant—stirruped trousers, a dark green military cap in Prussian style, a luxurious overcoat with a beaver collar. But despite all this, he seemed completely unpretentious. Ida muttered the name of one of Russia's most famous families, and he quickly took off his hat (it was lined, of course, with red *moire*), removed one of his white suede gloves to reveal a delicate, milky blue hand that felt as if it had been lightly dusted in flour, then clicked his heels together and respectfully lowered his painstakingly groomed head to his breast. 'What a sight!' the gentleman thought to himself, feeling even more amazed. He looked stupidly at Ida again and immediately understood from the glance she aimed at the student that she, of course, ruled his life, and the student was a slave—not at all an ordinary slave, however, but one who bore his bondage with utmost pleasure and even pride. 'I'm very, very glad to meet you,' the slave said with utter sincerity, lifting his head with a pleasant, cheerfull smile 'I'm a long-time admirer of yours, and Ida has told me a great deal about you,' he continued, looking at our hero affably. He was clearly ready to begin a conversation, but Ida cut him short. 'Be quiet, Petrik. Don't embarrass me,' she said hurriedly, turning to the gentleman. 'My dear, it's been a thousand years since I saw you. I'd like to talk endlessly, but not with him here. Our reminiscences will mean nothing to him. He'll be bored, and because of his boredom, we'll feel awkward. Let's go for a walk, instead.' And having spoken thus, she took our traveler by the arm and led him out of the station. They walked almost a full *verst* on the platform, where the snow was nearly knee-deep, and she suddenly confessed to being in love with him."

"What do you mean, in love with him?" we all asked at once. Instead of answering, the composer took another deep breath, filling his chest and straightening his shoulders. He lowered his eyes, then rose up clumsily in his seat. Ice rustled as he took a bottle from the silver tub and filled a wine glass with champagne. The skin over his cheekbones was flushed, and his short neck had turned red. Slouching in his seat, trying to hide his confusion, he drained his glass and began to sing once more with the phonograph—"*Laissez-moi, laissez-moi contempler ton visage! . . .*" but immediately broke off and resolutely looked at us with narrowed eyes:

"Yes, her love. . . . It was . . . her confession was, unfortunately, completely real and genuine. Sudden, stupid, absurd, unbelievable—yes, of course, it was all these things. But it remains a fact. Everything happened just as I am telling you. They walked onto the platform and right away she started talking quickly, started asking questions with contrived cheerfulness: How was Masha? How were their mutual friends in Moscow?

What was new in the city? Etcetera, etcetera. And then she announced that she had been married for more than a year, that she and her husband had spent some of that time in Saint Petersburg, some of it abroad, and the rest at their estate near Vitebsk. . . . The gentleman hurried along behind her, sensing, already, that something was wrong—that in a moment something stupid and unbelievable would occur—and he stared as hard as he could at the whiteness of the snow lying everywhere around them, heaped in endless drifts across the platforms and the rails, piled thickly on the roofs and the tops of all the red and green cars left standing on the tracks. He looked and with a terrible sense that his heart had gone still, he understood one thing: for years and years he had been completely, madly in love with this Ida. . . . You can imagine the rest of the story yourselves, I'm sure. It goes like this: Ida walked up to a row of crates left on some remote platform far from the station. She brushed the snow from one of the crates with her muff and sat down. She raised her slightly pallid face and her violet eyes toward the gentleman. And without the slightest pause, without the slightest warning, she said: 'Dearest, I want you to answer a question: Did you know that I was in love with you before? Do you know now that I'm in love with you still—that I've been in love with you for five entire years?'"

The music from the phonograph, which had been rumbling softly in the background, suddenly swelled into a grandiose, disturbing roar. The composer fell silent and raised his eyes to us—they seemed to be filled with fear and surprise.

"Yes," he continued quietly. "That's what she said to him. And now, let me ask you a question: How can one describe that moment with stupid human words? What can I tell you, other than cheap clichés, about that face turned toward him in the pallid light that only the snow of a recent storm produces? How can I describe that face which was itself as white as the snow, or the tender, ineffable emotions it expressed? How can I speak at all about the features of a beautiful young woman who walks in the snow and breathes the fresh, cold air, then suddenly stops to confess her love for you, and waits for you to respond? How did I describe her eyes? Violet? No, no—that's wrong, of course! And the way her lips were slightly parted? And the expression—the expression created by all her features combined—by her eyes, by her face and her lips? What can be said about the long sable muff in which her hands were hidden, or the outline of her knees beneath a checkered blue-green skirt? My God, who can even touch these things with words! And most important, most important—what answer could be given to that astounding confession which made him feel such dread and joy? What could he say as she trustingly looked up at him, waiting for an answer, her face drained of all color and distorted by a strange, uneasy smile?"

Not knowing how to respond, we stared with mute surprise at our companion's red face and glittering eyes. He answered his questions himself:

"Nothing, absolutely nothing. There are moments when a person must not make the slightest sound. And fortunately—to the great honor of our traveler—he said nothing at all. And she understood the way he froze before her, she saw his face. She waited there for a little while; she sat motionless in the absurd, cruel silence that followed her terrible question. And then she stood up, removed her warm, sweet-smelling hand from her muff, slipped it around his neck, and kissed him with both tenderness and passion. It was one of those kisses a man remembers not only on his deathbed but in the grave itself. And that was all—she kissed him and left. That's how the story ends. . . . And really, we've talked enough about this," the composer said, suddenly changing his tone. "In honor of my story, let's add to the fog in our brains," he continued loudly, trying to appear amused. "Let's drink to everyone who loved us and whom we—idiots that we are—didn't value. Let's make a toast to those who blessed us and made us happy and then were discarded forever from our lives, but remained forever linked to us by the most terrible link on earth. And let us agree, gentlemen, that I will smash this champagne bottle across the skull of anyone who adds even a single word to my story. Waiter!" he roared across the hall. "Bring the *ukha*! And sherry! A barrel of sherry! One big enough for a cuckold to douse his head with its horns!"

Our breakfast that day lasted until eleven at night. When it was over, we went to the Yar, and from there to the Strelna, where we ate *blinis* before dawn, ordered cheap vodka in bottles with red caps, and in general behaved scandalously: we shouted, sang, even danced the *kazachok*. The composer moved silently to the music—his dancing was violent, ecstatic, and surprisingly graceful for a man of his build. The morning sky was already pink when we raced home in the bitter cold. As our *troika* sailed past the Strastnoy Monastery, an icy, red sun rose from behind the roofs, and the first shuddering blow of the bells broke loose from the belfry—and all of frozen Moscow seemed to shake. The composer tore off his hat and with all his strength shouted tearfully across the square:

"My sun! My beloved! Hurrah!"

[1925]

Cranes

O<small>N A CLEAR</small>, cold day in late autumn, I'm driving at a steady trot down a big country road: low sun and brilliant light, bare fields, the expectant hush of fall. But then, in the distance behind me, I hear the sound of rattling wheels. I listen closely— it's the quick, shallow chatter of a light-running *droshky*. I turn and see that someone's gaining on me. Someone's drawing closer by the second—already his horse is clearly visible as it flies with all its strength down the road, and then the figure of a man emerges from behind: in brief snatches I see him covering the horse's back with blows from his whip and his reins. . . . Even as I wonder at this sight, he draws even with my coach; over the rattling wheels, I hear the horse's powerful breathing, and then a desperate cry: "To the side, sir! To the side!" Startled and amazed, I turn sharply from the road, and a beautiful bay mare flashes by: I see her eye, her flared nostril, new reins the color of sealing wax, a shiny new harness lathered with sweat from inside her thighs, and then a handsome, dark-haired *mouzhik*, who looks half-crazed from the reckless speed of his driving and some mindless, all-consuming mania. He gives me a furious glance as he passes, and I am struck by his brilliant red mouth; his fresh, tar-black beard; his new cap and the yellow silk shirt which he wears under an open black coat—I know him, I think to myself, it's the miller from near Livny—and already he's gone like the wind. He runs another *verst* down the road, then stops and jumps down from his *droshky*. I race after him, and drawing close, I see the horse standing in the middle of the road with her sides heaving, the sealing-wax reins hanging loose from the shaft, the driver face-down on the ground, the long flaps of his coat flung open.

"Sir," he shouts into the dirt. "Sir, the cranes!" He waves his arms in despair. "It's so sad! The cranes have flown away!" And shaking his head, he chokes on drunken tears.

[1930]

Caucasus

AFTER ARRIVING in Moscow, I furtively took a room in an inconspicuous guest house in an alley near the Arbat, and between our meetings, I lived like an anchorite, hungering for her. She came to me only three times during those days, saying, "I'm here for just a moment" as she darted into the room. The exquisite pallor of a woman filled with love and apprehension had blanched her skin. Her voice cracked when she spoke, and I was overwhelmed with tenderness and joy as she flung her umbrella on the floor, fumbled with her veil, hurried to embrace me.

"I think he suspects something," she said. "I think he knows something—he might have found the key to my desk and read one of your letters. You know how proud and cruel he can be. He's capable of anything when he's angry. He told me once straight out, 'I'll stop at nothing to defend my honor, the honor of a husband and an officer.' For some reason now he's begun to watch my every step—literally. I've got to be careful—extremely careful—for our plan to work. He's agreed to let me go—I convinced him I would die if I didn't see the south and the sea. But you, for God's sake—you must be patient."

It was a daring plan: take the same train together to the coast of the Caucasus and stay for three or four weeks in some utterly remote place. I knew that coast—I had lived a little while near Sochi when I was young and alone, and all my life I'd remembered autumn evenings among black cypresses and cold, grey waves. . . . She grew pale whenever I reminded her of this, and said, "But this time you'll be with me in that mountain jungle near the sea." We didn't believe our plan would come to life until the very last—it seemed too great a happiness.

Moscow was all mud and gloom. A cold rain fell as if summer had already ended and would not return; the streets glistened with the black umbrellas of pedestrians and the raised, trembling tops of horse-drawn cabs. As I drove through the dark, foul night to the train, everything inside me froze from fear and cold. I ran through the station with my hat pulled low over my eyes, my face buried in the collar of my coat.

The rain was pouring loudly over the roof of the small, first-class compartment that I'd reserved. I closed the window curtain; the porter wiped his hand on his white apron, took the tip I offered him, and went away. I locked the door behind him, parted the curtain, and sat completely still, my eyes fixed on the crowd flitting through the dim light of the station lamps as they hurried with their bags along the length of the train. To avoid a meeting on the platform, we'd agreed that I would come as early as I could and she as late as possible, but now it was time for her to arrive. I grew more and more alarmed—there was no sign of her. The second bell rang, and I shivered with fear: she'd missed the train, or he'd suddenly refused to let her go! But then I started at the sight of his tall figure, his officer's cap, his narrow overcoat, and the gloved hand with which he held her arm as he strode down the platform. I shrank into a corner of the berth and began to imagine how he would enter the second-class car behind mine, how he would inspect it all with an air of authority, how he would check whether the porter had arranged her well, how he would take off his hat, remove one suede glove, kiss her, make the sign of the cross. . . . I was stunned by the final bell; dazed by the first forward jerk of the train. It rocked and swayed from side to side as it pulled away; then the engine picked up speed and we were gliding smoothly down the rails. My hands were cold as ice when I gave ten rubles to the conductor who led her to me and carried in her bags.

She did not kiss me when she entered the compartment. Her hat had become tangled in her hair, and she smiled piteously as she sat down and struggled to remove it. "I couldn't eat," she said. "I was sure I wouldn't make it—sure I couldn't carry off this lie. . . . I'm desperately thirsty. Can you give me some Narzan?" she asked, addressing me for the first time with the familiar form of 'you.' "I know he'll come after me. I gave him two addresses—Gelendzhik and Gagry. And *voila*—he'll be in Gelendzhik in three or four days. But God be with him—death is better than this hell."

In the morning I went into the corridor, and it was full of sunlight. The stale air smelled of soap and cologne and all the other ordinary odors of daybreak on a crowded train. Through the hot, dusty windows I watched the steppe flow by. I saw the scorched stubble of the plains, oxen dragging carts down wide, dusty roads, and the metallic flash of the crossing-keepers' sheds, their gardens thick with scarlet mallow and sunflowers bright as canaries. The plain went on and on in all its emptiness: burial mounds and native graves under the dry, killing sun; the sky itself like a cloud of dust, and then, the rising ghosts of mountains.

She sent postcards from Gelendzhik and Gagry, telling him she didn't know where she would stay.

Then we started down the coast.

We found a pristine spot surrounded by plane trees and blooming shrubs, pomegranates, mahoganies and magnolias, black cypresses, palms with fan-shaped fronds.

I liked to get up early and follow the low hills far into the forest while she slept until seven, when we usually drank tea. The sun was already strong when I went out—clear, and full of joy. A fresh-smelling mist would slowly rise and burn in a blue radiance while I walked, the timeless white of mountain snow shining above the steep, wooded slopes. Returning home, I passed through the village bazaar, where the heat was already heavy, the air smelled of burning dung, and the crowd seethed around the merchants with their saddle horses and their mules. In the morning, different mountain tribes came down to the bazaar, and the Circassian women seemed to float along the ground in their long dark robes and red slippers, their heads wrapped in black fabric. Occasionally I'd see their eyes—fleeting, birdlike glances darting out from folds of mournful cloth.

Later we went to the beach, which was always empty, and swam and lay in the sun until lunch—fish cooked on a skewer

over an open fire, white wine, fresh fruit and nuts. In the after-
noons we closed the window shutters; joyful strips of light sloped
through their cracks into the warm twilight that gathered under
the tiled roof.

When the heat lifted and we opened our window, we could
see a portion of the sea between the cypresses that stood below
us. It was violet, and it lay so still that one could believe there
would be no end to this beauty, this peace.

At dusk, stunning clouds often drifted in from the sea, and
they burned so beautifully that she would lie on the ottoman
with a scarf of gauze across her face and weep: two weeks, maybe
three—then Moscow once again.

The nights were warm and thick. Fireflies drifted like topaz
in the murky dark; the songs of tree toads rang like small glass
bells. When our eyes adjusted, we could see stars and the mountain crest; trees we'd overlooked in daylight stood out sharply
above the village. All night the muffled beating of a drum rose
from the *dukhan,* mingling with howls of joy and hopelessness,
as if there were nothing but a single, endless song.

Near our house a clear, shallow stream flowed briskly down
a rocky ravine from the forest to the sea. How wonderfully the
falling water flashed, scattering itself like glass among the stones
at that secret hour when the late moon comes from behind the
mountains and the woods like a divinity, and looks down watch-
fully.

Sometimes at night terrible clouds moved down from the
mountains, and vicious storms began: again and again, a fantastic green abyss would suddenly appear and gape before us, then
vanish into the raging, mortal blackness of the forest, as thunder
split apart the sky like some primeval force. . . . Baby eagles
awoke in the rain and cried like cats, snow leopards roared, and

jackals yelped. Once an entire pack of jackals came to our lighted window—they were always drawn to buildings in the storms. We opened the window and looked down at them, and they stood in the shimmering downpour, yelping—as if they wanted us to let them in. She wept with joy as she watched.

He searched for her in Gelendzhik, Gagry, and Sochi. On the morning after his arrival in Sochi, he swam in the sea, shaved, put on a clean shirt and an officer's jacket that was white as snow. He had breakfast on the restaurant terrace at his hotel, drank a bottle of champagne and coffee with Chartreuse, slowly smoked a cigar. Then he went back to his room, lay down on the couch, put a pistol to each of his temples, and fired.

[1937]

The Hunchback's Affair

T HE HUNCHBACK received an anonymous love letter, an invitation to a rendezvous:

Come to the public garden on Cathedral Square on Saturday, April 5th, at seven in the evening. I am young, well off, and unencumbered, and—why hide it!—I have long known and loved you; your melancholy, proud expression; your intelligent and noble features; your loneliness. I would like to hope that in me you will find a soul kindred to your own. . . . I will be wearing a grey English suit; in my left hand I will carry a silk lavender umbrella; in my right a bouquet of violets.

How amazed he was! How he waited for the day! The first love letter of his life! On Saturday he went to the barber, bought a pair of lilac-colored gloves and a grey tie with a dash of red to match his suit. At home he dressed before a mirror, endlessly re-knotting that tie while his long, delicate fingers trembled and turned cold. An attractive flush had begun to spread across his cheeks, and his handsome eyes seemed to grow darker. . . . Then he sat down in an armchair, and like an impeccably dressed guest—like a stranger in his own house—he waited for the fateful hour. At last the dining room clock ominously chimed 6:30. He shuddered, then rose with composure, calmly put on his spring hat in the hallway, picked up his walking stick, slowly left the house. Once outside he could no longer restrain himself, however, and although his steps retained the proud solemnity that misshapen backs invariably produce, he moved his long, delicate legs more quickly than usual, seized by that blissful fear with which we all anticipate happiness. Hurrying into the garden by the cathedral, he suddenly froze: a woman was coming toward him in the pink light of the spring sunset. She walked with a certain stateliness, taking long, measured strides. She wore a grey suit and an attractive hat that slightly resembled a man's. She carried an umbrella in her left hand; in her right a bouquet of violets. And she too was a hunchback.

Someone has no mercy for man!

[1930]

Ballad

Before the big winter holidays our country home was always as hot as a sauna. The house consisted of spacious rooms with low ceilings, and we left all the doors inside wide open. It made a strange picture: one could see right through the house, from the entrance hall to the den, and every room glowed with the flames of lamps and wax candles that stood before the icons in the holy corners.

In preparation for those holidays the smooth oak floors of the house were carefully washed; they dried quickly in the heat, and then they were covered with clean horse cloths. The furniture that had been moved during the washing was meticulously rearranged in the rooms; the candles and lamps were lit before the icons in their gold and silver frames, and all the other lights were extinguished. By then the winter sky outside would be turning dark blue, and when we went to our separate rooms, full silence settled in the house—a reverential hush that seemed, somehow, to be waiting for another kind of peace. Nothing could have been more fitting among those icons and the mournful, tender light that played upon them in the dark.

Sometimes in the winter a wanderer named Mashenka stayed at the estate. She was a skinny, grey-haired old woman, as small as a young girl. She alone never slept during those nights: coming from the servants' quarters into the hall after dinner, she would remove her felt boots and softly walk along the horse cloths in her stocking feet, go soundlessly to every one of those rooms, kneel down in the heat and the mysterious light, cross herself and bow before each icon. Then she'd go back to the entrance hall to read prayers and psalms or simply talk to herself quietly while sitting on an old, black chest we'd kept there for years. It was by overhearing Mashenka's prayers that I learned of that sacred beast, "God's wolf."

Late one night when I was unable to sleep, I got up and started down the hall toward the den, where I hoped to find a book to read among those on the shelves. Mashenka didn't hear me; she was sitting in the dark foyer, saying something to herself. I stopped in the hall to listen—she was reciting psalms from memory:

"Lord, hear my prayer, listen to my cry," she said without expression. "Do not be unmoved by my tears, for I am your pilgrim and a stranger to this earth, like my fathers before me. . . .

"Speak, God: How terrible you are in your works!

"He who lives under the Lord's high roof, under your all-powerful protection is at peace. . . . You tread upon the asp and the serpent, flout the dragon and the lion. . . ."

She raised her voice softly but emphatically as she recited

the last words, pronouncing them with conviction: "flout the dragon and the lion." Then she fell silent for a moment, sighed, and said as if talking to someone else in the room: "For all the beasts in the forests and the cattle on the thousand hills are His."

I glanced into the foyer and saw her on the chest, her small feet in wool stockings held level above the floor, her arms crossed over her chest. She stared straight ahead without noticing me. Then she raised her eyes to the ceiling and said distinctly: "And you, sacred beast, God's wolf, pray for us to the heavenly mother."

I approached her and said softly, "Mashenka, don't be afraid, it's me."

She dropped her arms, stood, and made a low bow. "Hello, sir. I'm not afraid. What should I fear now? No, that was all childishness—being afraid. The dark-eyed devil confused me."

"Please, sit down," I said.

"No, sir, I'll stand, sir."

I laid my hand on her thin shoulder and her collarbone and made her sit beside me. "Please, if you won't sit down, I'll have to leave. Tell me, who were you praying to? Is there really such a saint—God's wolf?"

She tried to get up again; I held her down. "Wait, hold on. You say you aren't afraid of anything! I'm asking you—is there really a God's wolf?"

She paused, then answered solemnly. "There must be, sir. There is such a creature as the Tiger-Euphrates. And there was a picture of it in the church, so it must be so. I saw it myself, sir."

"How? Where did you see it? When?"

"A long time ago, sir—in a time older than memory. I can't even say where it was. All I remember is that we traveled there three days—a village called Krutye Gory. As you might know, sir,

I myself come from far away—I was born in Ryazan. This place was even farther south, beyond the Don. Such a primitive place, sir—you can't find words for it. The prince had been exiled there, but it came to be his favorite village—probably a thousand clay huts on the bare side of a mountain. Above them stood the manor house, a three-story building all exposed on the mountain peak over Stone River. Beside the house was a church with yellow walls and columns, and that sacred wolf's inside. In the middle of the church there's an iron slab over the grave of the prince he killed, and to the right there's a pillar where the wolf's painted, exactly as he appeared. His coat's grey and full, and he's leaning back on his hind legs, with his thick tail tucked under him. His front paws are pushing against the ground so that all his body seems to stretch and strain upward. He has a big head with sharp, pointed ears and a mane of grey fur around his neck. He stares at you with glowing eyes. His fangs are bared, and a golden light shines around his head, like the halo of a saint. It's terrible even to remember it, sir. He looks so real you think he's going to throw himself on you."

"Wait, Mashenka," I said. "I don't understand any of this. Who painted that wolf in the church? You say he killed the prince—then how can he be holy? And why is he beside the prince's tomb? And how did you wind up there, in that terrible village? Tell me everything in order."

And Mashenka began to explain:

"I wound up there, sir, because I was a serf at the time—as a girl I served in the household of a young prince. I was an orphan—they said my father was some kind of drifter, a runaway probably who seduced my mother and disappeared God knows where. My mother died soon after I was born, but the masters pitied me. They brought me from the servants' quarters into the household when I turned thirteen, made me an errand girl for the young lady of the house. She grew very fond of me for some reason and never let me out of her sight. So I went too when the young prince decided they should see the estate his grandfather had left him—it was that manor house in Krutye Gory. The estate had been deserted for years; it stood all empty and forgotten, abandoned after the grandfather's death. We'd all heard legends about the terrible way he died, and the young prince wanted to see the house for himself."

In the hallway something sizzled, then softly struck the floor. Mashenka jumped down from the chest and ran toward the noise: a candle had fallen, and we could smell something burning. Mashenka quickly put the candle out, stepped on the nap of the smoldering horse cloth, and then climbed onto a chair to relight the taper from those that still burned before the icon. As the candle flared up, she tipped it over and dripped wax like warm honey into the hole from which it had fallen; then she carefully reinserted the candle, trimmed the snuff from the others, and jumped down to the floor.

"Look how nicely it's all lit up," she said, crossing herself and glancing at the golden flames of the candles she'd revived. "The house feels like a holy place."

The rooms had filled with the sweet smell of burning wicks and wax. A saint stared out from a round silver frame behind the trembling flames of the candles. The bottom halves of the windows were covered in grey rime, but in the clear spaces above the frost I could see the night and the trees in the front garden; matted with snow, their sagging branches looked like the white paws of some strange animal. Mashenka glanced at them, crossed herself again, and came back to the foyer.

"It's time for you to rest, sir," she said as she sat back down on the chest and suppressed a yawn, covering her mouth with her small, bony hand. "This is when the night grows strict and cruel."

"Why do you say that?"

"Because this is a secret time, when only the rooster and the owl can keep awake. This is when the Lord himself listens to the earth, and the most important stars begin to play, and the ice holes freeze in the rivers and the oceans."

"Then why don't you sleep at night?"

"I sleep as much as I need to, sir. What good is sleep for an old person? We're like birds on a branch."

"Well, you should go to bed soon, all the same. But finish the story about the wolf."

"That's an old, dark business, sir. Maybe it was all just a ballad someone made up."

"What did you say?"

"A ballad, sir. All the prince's family talked about ballads. They liked reading them out loud. Sometimes I hear them and shivers run down my spine—

'The forest howls beyond the hills,
Wind rages in the chalk-white fields—
A storm has come,
The road is lost . . .'

Ah, it's wonderful!"

"What's wonderful about it?"

"It's wonderful because you can't say why it's wonderful. Because there's awe in it. Because it's terrifying."

"Everything was terrifying in the old days, Mashenka."

"What can I say, sir? Maybe you're right—maybe everything

was terrifying then, and I just remember wrong when it all seems dear and good. What was it really like? . . . So many tsars have passed, so many ancient trees have turned bare, so many graves grown level with the ground. . . . But here's how the story went—the serfs told it this way word for word—though who knows if it's true. It all took place during the reign of the Great Tsarina. She was actually the reason why he was in Krutye Gory—he'd angered her somehow, and she'd sent him as far away as possible from her. He grew savage in his exile—became a butcher of slaves and a rapist. He was still very strong and, as appearances go, very handsome. Apparently there wasn't a single girl among his household serfs or all his villagers he hadn't used—they had to spend a night with him before they married. And then he fell to the worst of sins: he began to lust for his own son's newlywed wife. The son had served in the army in Petersburg. When he found himself a bride, the father blessed the marriage and he, naturally, brought his new wife to meet his father in Krutye Gory. But the father soon wanted the girl himself. There's good reason, sir, for them to sing that love exists in every kingdom, that it warms all things on earth. And there's no sin in it, of course, if an old man just thinks about the girl he loves, and sighs. But this was not the same—the girl was like his own daughter, and he'd laid traps to get her in his bed."

"And what happened?"

"Well, the son, seeing what his father wanted, made plans to run away in secret. He bribed the stablemen, told them to harness a sleigh with three fast horses toward midnight. He came in secret from the house as soon as the old prince was asleep, called out his wife—and they fled. But the old prince wasn't asleep at all—he'd already heard everything from his spies and immediately tore off after his son.

"It was a dark, bitter night. The frost hung like a ring around the moon, and the snow was piled higher than a man could stand, but he doesn't feel a thing—he flies, flies on his horse with sabers and pistols in his belt, his favorite hounds-man galloping beside him. He sees the horses and the sleigh in the distance and shrieks like an eagle, 'Stop, or I'll shoot!' But they don't listen to him—they're driving as hard as they can. So the old prince starts to shoot. He kills the right trace horse in mid-stride, then he brings down the left trace. But as he takes aim at the shaft horse, he looks to his side and sees a great wolf in the moonlight, a wolf racing over the snow toward him: its eyes glow like red flames, and a golden light shines around its head! The old prince starts shooting at it, but the animal doesn't even blink. It rushes at him in a frenzy, leaps onto his chest, and in a flash tears out his throat with its fangs."

"Oh, how terrible Mashenka," I said. "It really is like a ballad!"

"It's a sin to laugh, sir," she answered. "Everything is possible with God."

"I won't argue with you, Mashenka. But it's still strange that they painted that wolf right beside the prince's tomb after he killed the man."

"He was painted there, sir, at the prince's own request. He was still alive when they got him home. He had time to repent before death and receive communion. And in his last moment he ordered that the wolf be painted beside his tomb in the church: a warning to his descendants. And who could deny his last request? The church was his, after all. He'd built it himself."

[1938]

First Class

ASUBURBAN TRAIN near Moscow—first- and second-class passengers only. It's been rolling steadily through the countryside, but now, suddenly, the train slows and something unheard of occurs: the conductor shoves a little *mouzhik* wearing clay-spattered rags into a first-class compartment.

"Forgive me, please, ladies and gentlemen," he says. "This worker has orders to go to Bykovo. He was supposed to ride with the engineer, but the fool didn't make it to the front of the train before we left. He'll only ride with you as far as Bykovo."

Everyone's astonished at first by this absurd situation. But the passengers keep calm, quickly recompose themselves. The train regains its speed, and the scene inside the compartment seems unchanged: the passengers smoke, converse, watch the scenery breeze by. But everyone's uncomfortable and out of sorts: the conversations are contrived, the cigarettes are smoked with fake insouciance. About the *mouzhik* there is nothing to say: he stands near the door, wishing the earth would open up and swallow him whole, hide him from these gentlemen in Tussore suits and Panama hats, these big, plump bodies and sated faces. He wipes the sweat from his forehead with one hand; with the other he holds a bag that stretches to the floor, weighted down with little iron bars, pliers, screws.

And it lasts a full thirty-five minutes, this torture, this nonsense.

[1930]

Cold Fall

IN JUNE of that year he was staying at our estate—we'd always considered him part of the family: his deceased father had been my father's friend and neighbor. On the 15th, Ferdinand was killed in Sarajevo; on the morning of the 16th, newspapers arrived in the mail. My mother and I were still drinking tea with him in the dining room when my father came from his study, the evening edition of a Moscow paper in hand.

"Well, friends," my father said. "It's war. The Austrian crown prince has been killed in Sarajevo. It is war."

On Saint Peter's day—my father's name day—many guests came to the house, and at lunch we announced our engagement. But on the 19th of July, Germany declared war on Russia.

In September he visited us for one more day to say goodbye before leaving for the front (everyone believed the war would end quickly; our wedding had been postponed until spring). And so began our last evening together. As usual, the samovar was brought into the dining room after dinner, and, watching the windows turn damp with its steam, my father said: "What a cold and early fall!"

The four of us sat quietly that evening and exchanged only a few meaningless words, concealing all our secret thoughts beneath an air of exaggerated calm. Even my father's words about the fall had been spoken with contrived simplicity. I went to the balcony doors, wiped the glass with my handkerchief, and looked out over the garden: sharp and icy stars were shining in the black sky. Leaning back in his armchair, my father smoked and stared absently at the hot lamp hanging over the table. In its light my mother wore her spectacles and carefully sewed a little silk pouch. Her work was both touching and terrible, for all of us knew what that pouch would hold.

"Do you still want to leave before breakfast?" My father asked.

"Yes, with your permission," he answered. "It's very sad, but I haven't taken care of everything at home."

My father sighed. "As you wish, my dear friend. But in that case, Mother and I must go to bed. We want to see you off in the morning. . . ."

Mother got up from her chair and made the sign of the cross over her future son. He bowed to her hand, and then to my father's. Left alone, we stayed a little while in the dining room— I played Patience distractedly at the table while he paced the floor.

"Would you like to take a little walk?" he asked.

Everything had turned heavy in my soul, and I answered with indifference. "Fine."

As we put on our coats in the hall, his thoughts seemed fixed on something far away. Then he smiled and recited from Fet: *"Such a cold fall! Put on your bonnet and your shawl."*

"I don't have a bonnet," I said. "But how does it go on?"

"I don't remember. Something like: *'Look—between the blackening pines / A fire has begun. . . .'"*

"What fire?"

"The moonrise, of course. There's something wonderful about that poem. You can really feel the charm of autumn in the countryside. . . . 'Put on your bonnet and your shawl' . . . That was our grandparents' time. . . . God . . . dear God!"

"Are you all right?" I asked.

"I'm fine, it's just . . . It's sad. Beautiful and sad. I love you very much."

Wearing our coats, we walked through the dining room to the balcony, then down into the garden. At first it was so dark that I held his sleeve, but then black branches revealed themselves in the mineral shine of the scattered stars. He stopped and turned toward the house.

"Look at the light in those windows. That kind of glow comes only in the fall. . . . If I live, I'll remember this night all my life."

As I turned to look, he put his arms around me. I pulled my scarf aside and leaned toward him. We kissed and he stood staring at my face.

"Your eyes are shining," he said. "Are you cold? It feels like winter out tonight. . . . If I'm killed, will you remember me a little while?"

And I thought: "What if he's right? If he's killed, could I forget him—is it possible with time? Isn't everything forgotten in the end?" And frightened by my thoughts, I blurted out: "Don't say that. I won't survive your death!"

He was silent for a moment. Then slowly he said: "Listen, if I am killed, I will wait for you there. Live your life, rejoice in this earth, then come to me."

Bitterly, I began to cry.

In the morning he left. Mother put that fateful pouch around his neck, the one she'd sewn the night before. It contained a small gold icon that her father and her grandfather had worn in war. As each of us made the sign of the cross over him, our arms seemed to jerk with despair. Then we fell into that stupor that always comes when people say goodbye before long separations. Watching him go, we felt nothing but an astounding sense of incongruity between ourselves and the joyful morning that surrounded us with sunlight and shimmering frost. We stood there for a little while and then went back into the empty house. I walked through all the rooms with my hands behind my back, not knowing if I should sob or sing at the top of my lungs.

He was killed—how strange the word seems!—a month later in Galicia. Thirty years have passed since then, and when I sort through that dream called the past—that dream neither our hearts nor our minds can comprehend—when I separate the years and turn them over one by one in memory, then I begin to recognize how long I've lived, how much has been survived. By the spring of 1918 both my parents were dead, and I was living in a basement owned by a woman who traded at Smolensky Market. She loved to laugh at me and scoff, "Well, your ladyship, how are your conditions?" as I too tried to survive in the marketplace by selling a ring or a cross or a collar of moth-eaten fur. Like so many others, I sold whatever I owned to soldiers who wore fur hats and strolled through the market with their great-coats unbuttoned. But somehow, on that corner where Smolen-sky intersects Arbat, I met an elderly, retired officer whose soul was rare and good. Soon we were married, and in April we left for Ekaterinodar with his nephew, a boy of seventeen who wanted to join the White Army. I dressed like a peasant woman and wore bast shoes; he put on a tattered Cossack coat, let his black and silver beard grow out—and for two weeks we traveled south until we reached the Don and the Kuban, where we stayed two years. And then, with countless other refugees, we set sail from Novorossysk for Turkey in a terrible winter storm: my hus-band died of typhus while we were still at sea. Of all the people on this earth, three remained who were close to me—my hus-band's nephew, his young wife, and their child, a baby girl of seven months. But the nephew and his wife soon left the child with me and joined Vrangel's regiment in the Crimea; there they disappeared without a trace. I lived a long time in Constantino-ple, supporting myself and the child through hard, demeaning work. And then, like so many others, we seemed to wander end-lessly. Bulgaria, Serbia, Bohemia, Belgium, Paris, Nice. . . . The girl grew up and stayed in Paris, became French and beautiful and utterly uninterested in me. She found a job in a chocolate store near the Madeleine—with well-groomed hands and silver, manicured nails, she deftly wraps packages in satin paper and ties them up with golden thread. But I've remained in Nice and live here still on whatever God provides. . . . I first saw Nice in 1912, and in those happy days I never could have dreamed of what this place would come to mean!

Thus I survived his death, having said so recklessly that I could not. But when I remember everything that I've been through, I always ask myself: What really was your life? And I answer: Only that cold autumn night. Did that night exist? It did. And that is all there was in my life. The rest is an unnecessary dream. And I believe, fervently believe: he is waiting for me somewhere there with all the love and youth he had that night. "You live your life, rejoice in this earth, then come to me." I have lived. I have rejoiced. And soon, soon I will come.

[1944]

Calf's Head

A FRECKLED five-year-old boy in a sailor's suit stands speechless at a butcher's stall, as if entranced. Father had to go to work at the post office, so mother took him with her to the market.

"We'll have calf's head with parsley today," she'd said to him, and he'd imagined something small and delicate sprinkled with bright green leaves.

So here he stands and looks, surrounded on all sides by something huge and red that hangs from rusty hooks to the floor, little stumps protruding from the joints where legs have been lopped off, and headless necks stretching to the ceiling. Among opalescent layers of fat, an empty stomach yawns at the front of each slab, and thin strips of rich meat shine with a pellucid film at the hip and shoulder bones. But the transfixed child stares only at the head, which happens to be lying on the marble counter directly in front of him. Mother is looking at the head as well, and arguing heatedly with the stall's owner. He too is huge and fleshy; his coarse white apron displays a sickening, rust-colored stain above his belly, and a heavy, greasy scabbard dangles from his low-slung belt. Mother's arguing about the head—just it, and nothing else. The owner shouts something angrily and pokes it with his soft finger. They are arguing about the head, but it lies motionless, indifferent. Its flat, bullish forehead is smooth and relaxed, the turbid blue eyes are half closed, the thick lashes look heavy with sleep. The nostrils, however, are flared, and the lips are so swollen that the head has a haughty, displeased expression. All of it's laid bare—the color of flesh going grey, resilient as rubber.

Then the butcher splits it down the middle with a terrifying blow from his axe and shoves one-half toward mother—one eye, one ear, one nostril flared on cotton-fiber paper.

[1930]

[63]

The Gentleman from San Francisco

T HE gentleman from San Francisco—no one really learned his name in Naples or Capri—was traveling with his wife and daughter to the Old World for two whole years, strictly for the sake of entertainment.

He was firmly convinced that he had every right to rest, enjoy himself, take a trip of utmost excellence in all regards. This conviction rested on two points: first, he was rich; second, despite his fifty-eight years, he had only just begun to live. He hadn't lived before—he had only existed. True, he had existed well, but always with his hopes put off to the future. He'd worked ceaselessly—the Chinese laborers whom he enlisted by the thousands understood exactly what that meant!—until at last, seeing that much had been accomplished and he'd drawn almost level to those he held as paragons, he decided it was time to rest. It was customary for his kind of people to begin enjoying life with trips to Europe, India, and Egypt—now he proposed to do the same. Of course, he wanted first and foremost to reward himself for all his years of work, but he was also happy for his wife and daughter. Although his wife's sensitivity to the world had never been particularly remarkable, all middle-aged American women love travel passionately, and for his daughter—a girl of poor health and increasing age—the trip was quite essential. After all, regardless of their beneficial health effects, don't such voyages often lead to happy meetings? One day you're dining or looking at a fresco, and right beside you there's a billionaire.

The gentleman from San Francisco worked out a vast itinerary. In December and January he would enjoy the sun of southern Italy, the ancient monuments, the *tarantella*, the songs of wandering minstrels, and that delicacy which people of his age were particularly well suited to appreciate in all its subtlety, even if it wasn't offered in a purely altruistic spirit: the love of Neapolitan girls. Carnival he planned to spend in Nice and Monte Carlo, where members of the most select society gather at that time of year, and one group ardently devotes itself to racing yachts and cars, another plays roulette, a third engages in a practice known as flirting, and a fourth shoots pigeons as they're released from cages, rising beautifully, for a moment, above the emerald lawns and the forget-me-not background of the sea, before plummeting in little white clumps to the ground. Early March he would devote to Florence, and for Holy Week they'd go to Rome to hear the *Miserere*. Venice, Paris, bullfighting in Seville, swimming off the British Isles—these were also in his plans, along with Athens, Constantinople, Palestine, Egypt, and even — on the journey home, of course — Japan. Everything went wonderfully at first.

It was the end of November, and they sailed through icy fogs or storms of wet snow all the way to Gibraltar. But they traveled comfortably. There were many passengers, and their ship, the renowned *Atlantis*, was like a huge hotel, with every comfort and convenience — a late-night bar, Turkish baths, even its own newspaper. Life on board flowed in perfect measure. They rose to bugle notes resounding sharply in the corridors at that early, gloomy hour when daylight was still spreading sullenly above the waves and the surging sea resembled a grey-green desert in the fog. They put on flannel pajamas, drank coffee and cacao or hot chocolate, bathed, did morning exercises in order to feel hungry and invigorated. Then they dressed and went to breakfast, after which it was customary to play shuffleboard and other games on deck or walk briskly around the ship, inhaling the cold freshness of the sea and stirring up an appetite again. At eleven the passengers fortified themselves with sandwiches and bouillon, and then, well fortified, they read the newspaper with pleasure or waited patiently for lunch, which was even more filling and diverse than breakfast. The two hours following their second meal were set aside for resting: wrapped in warm blankets, the passengers lay on cane-back couches specially arranged along the decks, dozing peacefully or staring at the cloudy sky and the foaming swells that flashed beyond the ship's sides. Some time after four, feeling cheerful and refreshed, they were given cookies and strong, fragrant tea; and at seven, trumpet notes announced the key event of their existence — its crowning glory: immediately the gentleman from San Francisco would hurry to his wealthy cabin in order to get dressed.

Evenings, the many portals of the *Atlantis* shone like countless glowing eyes in the gloom while a vast multitude of servants
labored below deck in the galleys, the sculleries, and the wine
cellars. The ocean passing outside the walls was terrifying to
them, but they rarely thought of it, believing firmly in the powers
of their captain, a red-haired man of monstrous height and
weight who always seemed slightly sleepy, rarely left his secret
cabin, and resembled a massive pagan idol in his uniform with
broad gold stripes across its sleeves. Every few minutes, a siren on
the forecastle would yelp as if enraged and start to howl with des-
olate despair, but few passengers could hear it: an orchestra
played ceaselessly in the festive, two-toned dining room, and the
delicate sound of its strings drowned out the siren's wailing while
throngs of women in revealing gowns and men in tails and dinner jackets were served by trim waiters and obliging *maitre d's*,
one of whom wore a little chain around his neck like a lord
mayor and specialized exclusively in wines.

His starched white linen and his dinner jacket made the
gentleman from San Francisco look younger than his age. Short
and slightly withered, strongly built but somehow ill propor-
tioned, he sat in the golden, pearly light of the hall with a bottle
of wine, goblets of the finest glass, and a rich bouquet of hy-
acinths before him. There was something Mongolian about his
sallow face and neatly trimmed silver moustache. His large teeth
gleamed with gold fillings, and the outlines of a strong, hard
skull were visible beneath his hairless scalp, which glistened like
old ivory. His wife, a large woman with wide hips and a peaceful
disposition, was dressed expensively but in keeping with her
years. Tall and thin, his daughter wore a light, transparent, elaborate, and revealing dress with innocent immodesty, her splendid

hair charmingly arranged, her breath freshened by the scent of violet lozenges, a few pink and tender pimples near her lips and between her lightly powdered shoulder blades.

Dinner lasted for more than an hour; then dancing began in the ballroom, and the men—including, of course, the gentleman from San Francisco—put their feet up in the bar, smoked Havana cigars, and drank liquor until their faces were as red as beets while being waited on by Negroes in red waistcoats, their bulging eyes like large, peeled eggs. The ocean's massive black hills boomed beyond the walls, a blizzard whistled shrilly in the burdened rigging, and the entire ship shuddered as it forged through the storm and those hills—like a plow it parted the ocean's seething mass, toppling the waves onto their sides as they boiled and rose and flung huge tails of foam high into the air. Muffled by the fog, the siren moaned in dire misery, the men on watch began to freeze and grow hysterical from the overwhelming strain of following the storm, and in the underwater belly of the ship, which resembled hell's ninth and final circle with its hot, dark depths, huge furnaces cackled indistinctly, consuming mounds of coal flung roaring into their molten jaws by men stripped to the waist, their bodies streaked with soot and acrid sweat, purple in the light of the flames. But there in the bar, men casually draped their legs over the armrests of their chairs, savoring their cognac and liquor while their heads grew light in pungent clouds of cigar smoke. In the warm and joyful ballroom, everything was flooded with bright light; the couples spun through waltzes or bowed and swayed to tangos, and with sweet shamelessness the music continued its sad, insistent pleading— always its entreaties were the same. The brilliant crowd included a great tycoon who was tall, clean-shaven, and dressed in old-fashioned tails; a celebrated Spanish writer; a world-renowned beauty; and a graceful, loving couple whom everyone observed with curiosity. The two of them made no effort to conceal their happiness as he danced exclusively with her, and everything they did was so delicate and charming that no one but the captain knew they'd been well paid by Lloyds to feign their love and sail on different ships for years.

In Gibraltar the sun made everyone happy: it felt like early spring, and a new passenger appeared on the deck of the *Atlantis*, attracting universal interest. A small, wooden man with a wide face and narrow eyes behind gold-rimmed glasses, he was the crown prince of some Asian country, traveling incognito. There was something disconcerting about the long, sparse strands of his moustache, which—like the facial hair of a corpse—revealed the skin above his lip, but the prince was generally quite pleasant, very modest, down-to-earth, and kind. In the Mediterranean they sailed among large waves as colorful as peacock tails, which the *tramontana* blew apart with savage glee as it rushed head-on toward the ship beneath a cloudless, brilliant sky. And then, on the second day, the sky began to whiten and a cloudiness appeared on the horizon: they were approaching land. Ischia and Capri came into view, and with binoculars one could see Naples scattered like sugar cubes at the base of a blue-grey mass. Many gentlemen and ladies had already donned light winter coats trimmed with fur while the cabin boys—soft-spoken, timid Chinese teenagers with bowed legs, coal black braids that reached their heels, and thick, girlish eyelashes—unhurriedly began to carry suitcases, walking sticks, blankets, and overnight bags to the stairs. The gentleman from San Francisco's daughter stood on deck beside the prince, who'd been introduced to her by lucky happenstance the night before, and pretended to look intently at something he was pointing out in the distance. He was explaining something, telling a story quietly and quickly, but the girl was so excited that she listened without understanding any of the words he spoke. With his spectacles, his bowler, and his English overcoat, the prince looked truly odd and unattractive. He was no taller than a boy; the strands of his moustache resembled horsehair; and the dark, delicate skin across his level face seemed to have been pulled taut and lightly varnished. But in his presence the girl's heart throbbed with inexplicable ecstasy: everything, everything about him—his dry hands, his clear skin, his ancient royal blood—made him unlike any other, and even his remarkably neat but simple European clothes seemed to hide some secret charm. Meanwhile, the gentleman from San Francisco, who had donned grey spats, was looking at the world-renowned beauty—tall and blond, with a surprising build and eyelids painted in the latest Paris fashion, she stood nearby, talking to a tiny, scruffy, bow-backed dog, which she held on a silver chain. Vaguely embarrassed, the gentleman from San Francisco's daughter made an effort not to notice her father.

He'd been quite generous on the journey and therefore had no doubts about the solicitude of those who'd given him food and drink, anticipated his slightest whim from morning until night, preserved his cleanliness and peace, carried his possessions, called for porters, delivered all his luggage to hotels. It had been this way everywhere he went; it had been this way on board the ship, and it would be this way in Naples. Naples was growing large and drawing close; with their brass instruments gleaming in the sun, musicians had already gathered on the deck, and now a festive marching song deafened the crowd. The giant captain appeared in full uniform on the bridge and waved graciously to the passengers, like a beneficent god. And when the *Atlantis* finally entered port with throngs of passengers spread among its decks, when its massive, multistoried frame gently pulled alongside the dock and the gangplanks dropped with a bang, what a crowd of porters and their assistants wearing peaked, gold-braided hats, what a crowd of assorted salesmen and whistling boys and robust urchins with packs of colored postcards in their hands rushed toward him, offering their services! But the gentleman from San Francisco only smirked at them as he approached a car dispatched from a hotel where royalty might stay, and calmly repeated through his teeth in English and Italian: "Go Away! *Via!*"

Life in Naples quickly fell into a set routine: early morning breakfast in the gloomy dining room; a cloudy, discouraging sky and a crowd of tour guides near the vestibule doors; the first smiles of a warm and pinkish sun; a moment on the high balcony, where one could see Vesuvius still fully cloaked in a shimmering haze, the silver-pearly ripples of the bay, the delicate outline of Capri on the horizon, and lower down, tiny donkeys pulling two-wheeled carts along the shoreline at a trot, little regiments of soldiers marching off somewhere to upbeat, rousing music; then the leaving for the car; the slow ride through damp and crowded streets that wound like narrow corridors among tall buildings with many windows; a tour of some lifelessly clean museum where the light was pleasant, flat, and dull, like the light that rises from snow; or a visit to another cold cathedral, where always it was the same: a majestic entrance covered by a heavy leather curtain, beyond which one discovered a huge emptiness; silence and the smell of burning wax; the quiet, red little flames of a seven-branched candelabrum on a distant altar adorned with lace; a lonely old woman among the dark wooden pews; slick tombstones underfoot; and another invariably renowned rendition of Christ's descent from the cross. At one o'clock they lunched on San Martino, where many first-class people could be found midday, and where the gentleman from San Francisco's daughter almost fainted after thinking that she saw the prince sitting in the hall, even though she knew from the newspapers that he was touring Rome. At five they had tea in the elegant drawing room of their hotel, warmed by carpets and a blazing fireplace; and then, once more, preparations for the evening meal began: again the imperious crashing of a gong on every floor; again the lines of women in revealing gowns, the rustling of silks as they descended the stairs, the reflections of their figures in the mirrors as they passed; again the welcoming, palatial dining room, the red jackets of musicians on a little stage, and the black uniforms of waiters gathering around a *maitre d'*, who with unmatched artistry ladled thick, pink soup into the dinner bowls. And again the meals were so rich and varied, there was so much wine and mineral water, so many sweet desserts and so much fruit that some time near eleven the maids would bring hot-water bottles to the rooms so that all the guests could warm their burdened stomachs.

All the same, December wasn't perfect: when discussing the weather, the porters only shrugged their shoulders guiltily and claimed that no one could remember such a year, although this was not the first time they'd had to mutter such phrases and allude to something terrible occurring everywhere: unheard of storms and downpours in the Riviera; Athens under snow, and such big drifts on Aetna that the mountain shined at night; tourists abandoning Palermo to escape the freezing cold. . . . The morning sun deceived them every day: by afternoon the sky invariably turned grey and a light rain began to fall, quickly turning cold and heavy. Then the palms outside the hotel entrance glistened like wet tin; the town seemed especially crowded and dirty, the museums exceedingly monotonous. On those rainy after-noons, the rubber cloaks of fat cabbies fluttered in the wind like wings, the stench of their cigar butts became unbearable, and the energetic whip-blows they delivered to the air above their wretched, thin-necked nags looked absurdly fake. There was something terrible about the shoes of the *signori* who swept the trolley tracks during those showers, something offensive and absurd about the short legs of the women who slopped through the mud, their dark hair uncovered in the rain. And about the dampness, about the stink of rotting fish that rose from the foamy sea along the shoreline, there was simply nothing to be said.

The gentleman from San Francisco and his wife began to quarrel in the mornings. Their daughter was either pale and troubled by an aching head or wildly animated and enthusiastic about everything she saw. At such moments she was particularly sweet and beautiful—as were those complex, tender feelings that her meeting with an ugly man whose veins contained rare blood had stirred in her, for in the end it doesn't matter if it's money, glory, fame, or lineage that stirs a young girl's soul. . . . Everyone assured them that things were different in Sorrento and on Capri: it was warm and sunny there, they said, and all the lemon trees were blooming; the locals were more honest, the wine more natural. Thus the travelers from San Francisco decided to set out with all their trunks and luggage for Capri, so that after they'd explored the island—walked around the ruins of Tiberius's palaces, visited the caves of the fantastic Azure Grotto, and listened to the bagpipes of those Abruzzian highlanders who roam the island singing praises to the Virgin Mary for a full month leading up to Christmas—they could begin their stay in Sorrento.

On the day of their departure—a day the family from San Francisco would remember well—there was no sun at all, even in the morning. A heavy fog blanketed Vesuvius and hung low over the lead-grey ripples of the sea. Capri was completely hidden from view—it seemed that such a place had never existed on this earth—and the small steamer bound for the island rocked so violently from side to side that the family from San Francisco lay motionless on the couches in the tiny passengers' lounge, their legs wrapped in blankets and their eyes pressed shut from nausea. The gentleman from San Francisco's wife believed she was suffering the most; indeed, the certainty that she was dying overcame her several times. But the ship's attendant—a woman who had tirelessly endured such waves for years in both the freezing cold and the scorching heat—merely laughed as she ran toward her with a bowl. Terribly pale, the daughter traveled with a slice of lemon held between her teeth, and the gentleman from San Francisco never once unclenched his jaw as he lay on his back in a long overcoat and a large, peaked cap, his head throbbing, his face darkening, and his moustache turning white: lately the bad weather had led him to drink too much in the evenings and to enjoy too frequently the *tableaux vivants* of certain haunts. Rain beat against the rattling windowpanes and dripped onto the couches; the wind howled as it tore through the masts and from time to time, in combination with a sudden, rising wave, set the small steamer completely on its side, at which point something crashed and rolled around the cargo space below the passengers. During stops in Castellammare and Sorrento there was some relief, but the ship continued pitching violently, and everything on shore—the cliffs and gardens; the Italian pines and pink and white hotels; the smoky, leafy hills—flew up and down outside the window like something on a swing. Boats banged against the walls, a damp wind blew through the open doors, and there was no reprieve from the constant, slightly garbled, piercing shouts of the boy who stood beneath a banner for the Hotel Royal on a rocking barge nearby and exhorted all the passing travelers to join him. Fittingly enough, the gentleman from San Francisco felt like a very old man, and he thought with bitter misery about those greedy little garlic-eaters called Italians who surrounded him. During one of the stops he rose up on the couch, opened his eyes, and saw a wretched mass of little stone houses with mildewed walls stacked on top of one another at the water's edge below a rocky slope, saw boats and piles of rags, tin cans, brown nets—and fell into despair, remembering that this was the authentic Italy to which he'd come in order to enjoy himself. It was already dusk when the island began to draw closer, like a black mass pierced by little red lights at its base. The wind settled down, grew warm and fragrant, the waves flowed like black oil, and wide bands of golden light snaked across their surface from the pier. . . . Then the anchor rattled on its chain and splashed into the water; the eager shouts of boatmen vying for passengers resounded from all directions; and immediately their spirits rose: the cabin seemed brighter, they felt like eating, drinking, moving once again. Ten minutes later the family from San Francisco boarded a big barge; five minutes after that, they climbed the stone embankment on the shore and entered a bright cable car that carried them up the mountainside, droning as it passed over the staked grapevines in the vineyards, half-collapsed walls of stone, and wet, gnarled orange trees, sheltered here and there by awnings made of straw—all of which slid slowly down the incline, the oranges shining, the broad leaves glistening as they drifted past the open windows of the car. The earth smells sweet in Italy after rain, and the scent of every island is distinct.

The island of Capri was dark and damp that evening. But now it came to life, grew light in places. Already a crowd had gathered on the little platform where the cable car would stop on the mountain top—a crowd of people charged with meeting the gentleman from San Francisco in proper fashion. There were other passengers as well, but they didn't warrant much attention—a few disheveled, bearded Russians who had settled on the island, all of them wearing glasses and looking absentminded, the collars raised on their threadbare coats; and a group of German youths with remarkably long necks and very round heads: dressed in Tyrolean suits and wearing canvas bags on their backs, they clearly had no need of assistance and were wholly unprepared to pay for it. The gentleman from San Francisco calmly kept his distance from both groups, and the waiting crowd soon noticed him. He and his women were hurriedly assisted from the car, people ran ahead to show them the road, and the gentleman from San Francisco was surrounded once again by boys and those robust peasant women who carry the suitcases and trunks of respectable tourists on their heads. Their wooden shoes tapped across the little square, which resembled an opera stage with one electric bulb swaying above it in the damp wind; the crowd of boys whistled like birds and did somersaults—and as if he were part of some performance, the gentleman from San Francisco walked among them toward a medieval arch below a group of buildings that had merged into one structure, and there, a little echoing street sloped toward the hotel's shining entrance, a palm tree with its fronds hanging like a forelock over the flat roofs to the left, dark blue stars in the black sky overhead. And it seemed that all of this was in honor of the guests from San Francisco—it seemed this damp, stony little town on the cliffs of an island in the Mediterranean had come to life on their account; that they alone made the hotel's owner happy and content, and the Chinese gong that began to ring on every floor the moment they arrived had been waiting all this time for them before summoning the guests to dinner.

The hotel's owner, a remarkably elegant young man who greeted the family with a refined and courteous bow, startled the gentleman from San Francisco: suddenly he remembered that among the senseless dreams that had beleaguered him all night, he'd seen this very gentleman, exactly him, with the very same morning coat, the very same hair combed to a mirrorlike sheen. Surprised, he almost faltered in his steps. But since every trace of so-called mysticism had long ago been eradicated from his soul, his amazement quickly passed, and he told his wife and daughter lightheartedly of the strange coincidence as they walked along the corridor. But his daughter looked at him with alarm when he spoke: suddenly her heart was gripped with sorrow and a terrifying loneliness on that strange, dark island. . . .

An important figure, Prince Reus XVII, had very recently checked out of the hotel; now his suites were given to the family from San Francisco. And the new guests were served by the most striking steward, a coal-black Sicilian with fiery eyes; the most able and attractive of the chambermaids, a Belgian who wore a starched white cap resembling a crown with little teeth and a corset that kept her waist firm and thin; and the very best of bellhops, the short and plump Luigi, who in his time had worked in many fine establishments. Soon the French *maitre d'* knocked lightly on the door of the gentleman from San Francisco's suite: he'd come to ask if the new guests would dine and, in the event he should receive an affirmative answer—of which, of course, he had no doubt—to inform the gentleman that tonight rock lobster would be served, along with pheasant and asparagus, roast beef, and so on. That wretched little Italian steamer had so thoroughly discomposed the gentleman from San Francisco that the floor still seemed to sway beneath his feet, but he didn't falter as he reached out with his own unpracticed, slightly awkward hand and closed the window that had banged open upon the *maitre d'*s entrance, momentarily releasing into the room the smell of cooking smoke from the distant kitchen, the scent of wet flowers from the garden. And he answered with leisurely precision that the family would dine, that their table should be set far back from the entrance, that they would drink the local wine—and in response to each of his words, the *maitre d'* made little sounds of assent in varying intonations, all of which were intended to express the thought that there could be no doubt about the absolute correctness of the gentleman's desires, and that everything would be fulfilled precisely as he ordered. Then the *maitre d'* tilted his head at a slight angle and politely asked, "Is that all, sir?"

And having received a drawn-out "yes" in answer to his question, he added that the *tarantella* would be performed that evening in the hotel vestibule by Carmella and Giuseppe, who were famous throughout Italy and "the entire tourist world."

"I saw her on the postcards," the gentleman from San Francisco said in a voice devoid of all expression. "That Giuseppe, is he her husband?"

"Her cousin, sir," answered the *maitre d'*. And after pausing for a moment, after contemplating something silently, the gentleman from San Francisco released him with a nod.

And then he started getting ready once again, as if preparing for a wedding. He turned on all the lamps, flooded every mirror with reflected light and glare, images of furniture and open trunks; he began to shave and wash and ring the bell for the attendant constantly, competing all the while with equally impatient calls that rang out from his wife and daughter's rooms. Grimacing with horror, Luigi raced toward each ringing bell with that lightness that many people who are fat possess, and all the maids running down the corridors with porcelain jugs in their hands laughed so hard they almost cried as he tore past them in his red apron, rapped lightly with his knuckles on the door, and in a voice so full of feigned timidity that it bordered on the imbecilic, asked: "*Na sonata, Signore?*"

And from behind the door, a slow, rasping, and insultingly decorous voice replied: "Yes, come in."

What did the gentleman from San Francisco think and feel that evening, which was so significant for him? Like anyone recovering from seasickness, he simply wanted very much to eat, and he imagined with great pleasure the first spoonful of soup, the first swallow of wine. These thoughts excited him so much that he finished his preparations for the meal in a somewhat agitated state, which left no time for any other feelings or reflection.

Having shaved and washed and comfortably inserted his false teeth, the gentleman from San Francisco stood before the mirror with several dampened silver brushes and straightened the last pearly strands of hair across his dark yellow scalp; stretched a pair of silk, cream-colored briefs over his strong, old man's body with its waist grown large from overeating; and slipped his flat, withered feet into black silk socks and evening shoes. He briefly bent his knees in order to adjust his black pants, held high by silk suspenders, and to straighten out his billowing, snow-white shirtfront; then he adjusted the cuff links at the edges of his brilliant sleeves and began struggling to fasten the top stud on his stiff collar. The floor still rocked beneath him, his fingertips throbbed, and the stud bit painfully into the loose, thin skin lying in a little recess just below his Adam's apple. But he persisted, and at last—his eyes shining from the effort, his face a bluish-grey from the exceedingly tight collar that now constricted his throat—the gentleman from San Francisco completed his toilet and sat exhausted before the pier glass, his reflection multiplied by all the other mirrors that surrounded him.

"Oh, this is awful," he muttered, lowering his bald head and making no attempt to contemplate exactly what was awful. Out of habit, he began to carefully inspect his short fingers: their stiffened, gouty joints; their large and prominent almond-colored nails. "This is awful," he repeated with conviction.

But just then the second gong rang out like something in a pagan temple, and the gentleman from San Francisco quickly rose. He pulled his collar even tighter with his tie, girded his stomach even more firmly with his waistcoat, donned his dinner jacket, straightened his cuff links, looked at himself in the mirror again. . . . "That Carmella," he thought, "there's something kittenish about her eyes. And such dark skin. She looks like a mulatto, especially in that bright orange costume. I bet her dancing is extraordinary." Cheerfully he left the room, walked along the carpet to his wife and daughter's suites, and asked in a loud voice if they'd be ready soon.

"In five minutes," a girl's voice rang out happily and clearly from behind the door.

"Excellent," said the gentleman from San Francisco.

Then he leisurely set out along the corridors and the red-carpeted stairs, looking for the reading room. Servants whom he met quickly turned away and pressed themselves against the wall—he passed as if not seeing them. And he quickly overtook an old woman who, late for dinner, was doing all she could to hurry down the hall: she wore a low-cut evening gown of light grey silk, but her hair was white as milk, her back was hunched, and all her efforts to move quickly only had a comical effect, for she looked like a bustling chicken. Near the glass doors of the dining room, where all the guests had already gathered and begun to eat, he stopped before a table loaded down with Egyptian cigarettes and boxes of cigars, picked out a large Manila, and tossed down three lire. Crossing the winter veranda, he glanced at an open window: a gentle breeze from the darkness passed over him; he saw the top of an old palm tree, vague as something in a dream with its huge fronds spread among the stars; the unfaltering sound of the distant sea reached his ears. . . . A grey-haired German who resembled Ibsen with his round, silver-framed glasses and his crazy, startled eyes stood leafing through a newspaper in the comfortable and quiet reading room, where the only lamplight lay neatly on the tables. The gentleman from San Francisco looked him over coldly, then settled into a plush leather armchair in the corner near a lamp with a green shade, placed his pince-nez on the bridge of his nose, craned his neck away from his suffocating collar, and disappeared completely behind his newspaper. He skimmed a few headlines, read a few sentences about the endless Balkan War, turned the page just as he always did—and suddenly the lines of newsprint flashed like glass before him, his neck went taut and his eyes bugged out, the pince-nez flew from his nose. . . . He lunged forward, tried to draw a breath, and snorted violently. His jaw dropped open, and his mouth filled with the golden glow of light reflected from his fillings. His head fell to his shoulder and began to roll from side to side; his shirtfront jutted out, as if a shoebox had been thrust beneath it, and his entire body writhed as he slid to the floor, digging at the carpet with his heels, struggling with someone desperately.

If the German hadn't been inside the reading room, the

hotel staff would have quickly and discreetly put an end to this unpleasant display; they would have grabbed the gentleman from San Francisco by his head and feet and quietly hauled him out the back, and not a single guest would have known what he'd been up to in the reading room. But the German burst into the hallway with a shout, roused the entire building and the dining room. Guests jumped up from their meals and ran into the reading room, turning pale. "What? What happened?" they asked in every language, and no one answered their murmuring, for even to this day death astounds us more than anything, and no one wants to believe in it. The owner rushed around among the guests, trying to stop them as they ran into the room, and to calm them down with hurried assurances that it was nothing at all — just a fainting spell suffered by a certain gentleman from San Francisco — but no one listened to him, and many saw how the stewards and the bellhops tore off the gentleman's tie, his waistcoat, his crumpled jacket, and even, for some reason, pulled the evening shoes from his flat feet in their black silk socks. And he was still fighting: he struggled stubbornly with death, refusing to submit to such a crude and unexpected attack. He shook his head and snorted like an animal at slaughter, rolled his eyes like a drunk. . . . When they hurriedly carried him away to a bed in room 43 — the hotel's smallest, coldest, dampest room, which stood at the end of the ground-floor corridor — his daughter came running, her hair undone, her half-uncovered breasts raised high by a corset, and then his heavy-set wife arrived, fully dressed for dinner, her mouth round with horror. . . . But the gentleman from San Francisco had already stopped shaking his head.

Fifteen minutes later some semblance of order had been restored in the hotel. But the evening was damaged beyond repair. Some of the guests returned to the dining room to finish their meals, but they all ate silently and looked offended while the owner, who felt to blame despite his innocence, went from one table to another, shrugging his shoulders with just the right degree of helpless indignation, assuring everyone he understood perfectly "how unpleasant" this had been, and promising to use "all means at his disposal" to correct the situation. They were forced to cancel the *tarantella*, and all the extra lights were turned off. Most of the guests went to a tavern in town, and it grew so quiet in the hotel that one could clearly hear the clock ticking in the vestibule, where a parrot muttered something woodenly to itself in its cage, fidgeting as it senselessly contrived to sleep with one foot awkwardly raised on its upper roost. . . .

The gentleman from San Francisco lay on a bed of cheap cast iron, light from one electric bulb falling dimly on the coarse wool blankets wrapped around his body. An ice bag sagged on his damp, cold forehead. His lifeless, blue-grey face was gradually stiffening, and the rasping, gurgling sound of his breath was weakening as it rose from his open mouth, where a golden light still glimmered. And already it was not the gentleman from San Francisco who snored, it was someone else, for the gentleman from San Francisco was gone. His wife and daughter, a doctor, and some servants stood and watched. And then the thing they'd feared and waited for with dread took place: the wheezing stopped. And slowly, slowly, before the eyes of all who watched, a pallor spread across the dead man's face while his features lightened and grew finer. . . .

The owner came in. "*Gia e morto*," the doctor told him in a whisper. The owner's face remained impassive; he shrugged his shoulders. Tears quietly rolling down her face, the gentleman from San Francisco's wife approached him and said timidly that it was time to return her husband to his suite.

"Oh no, Madame," the owner objected quickly and correctly. He spoke French, instead of English, and his voice lacked all its former courtesy, for he had no interest in the trifles that these visitors from San Francisco would now leave inside his register. "That's utterly impossible, Madame," he said, explaining that if he carried out her wish, all Capri would learn of it, and future tourists would refuse those rooms, which he valued very highly.

The daughter, who'd been looking at him strangely while he spoke, sat down in a chair, pressed a handkerchief to her mouth, and began to sob. The wife's tears dried immediately. An angry look flashed across her face; she raised her voice and began to make demands, speaking her own language, refusing to believe that all respect for them was lost for good. But the owner silenced her with dignified civility: if Madame did not care for conditions in the hotel, he had no right to detain her. And then he added sternly that the body must be removed today at dawn, that the police had been informed of the situation, and that their representative would soon arrive to complete the necessary formalities. . . . Could they at least find a simple coffin for sale on Capri? the Madame asked. Unfortunately, that was quite impossible; and no one would have time to make one. They would have to take some other course of action. . . . English soda water, for example, was delivered to the hotel in long, large boxes. . . . The dividers could be taken out. . . .

All the guests had gone to sleep. In room 43 they opened a window—it looked out onto a corner of the garden, where a sickly banana tree stood beside a high stone wall topped with broken glass—turned out the lights, locked the door, and left. The dead man remained in darkness; dark blue stars looked down on him from the sky. A cricket on the wall began to chirp with melancholy aimlessness. . . . Two maids sat on a windowsill, darning in the dimly lit corridor. Luigi approached them, wearing slippers, a stack of dresses slung over one arm.

"*Pronto?*" he asked in an anxious voice, casting his eyes toward the frightful door at the end of the hall. He gently waved his free hand in that direction. "*Partenza!*" he shouted in a whisper, as if seeing off a train—for this is what they shout in Italy as the cars begin to move—and the maids dropped their heads on one another's shoulders, choking on their stifled laughter.

Then he softly skipped down the hall to the door itself, knocked lightly, cocked his head to one side, and asked in the most courteous whisper:

"*Na sonata, Signore?*"

And constricting his throat, thrusting out his lower jaw, he answered himself in a drawn-out, sad, and rasping voice that seemed to come from behind the door: "Yes, come in."

At dawn, while it grew white outside room 43; while a damp wind rustled the torn leaves of the banana tree and a light blue morning sky rose and spread out over the island of Capri; while the clear, precise peak of Mount Solaro turned golden in the sun as it ascended over the distant blue mountains of Italy, and the masons who repair stone paths for tourists on the island left for work, a long box for English soda water was carried to room 43. Soon the box became very heavy, and it pressed hard against the knees of the junior porter who rode beside it in a horse-drawn cart, quickly descending to the sea along a white highway that wound back and forth among the slopes and stone walls and the vineyards of Capri. The driver, a scrawny little man in worn-out shoes and an old, short-sleeved jacket, had been playing dice all night in a cheap café, and now, red-eyed and hung over, he incessantly whipped his small, strong horse, who was adorned Sicilian style with little bells that jingled earnestly on the points of his bronze-plated saddle-strap pad and on his bridle, among pompoms of bright wool, while a yard-long feather, rising from the horse's clipped forelock, trembled as he trotted down the road. The driver sat silently, weighed down by thoughts of his bad habits and his dissipation, and by the fact that he'd lost his last lira the previous night. But the morning was fresh, and in such air—surrounded by the sea, beneath the morning sky—the haze of a hangover quickly clears, an easy calm comes back, and the driver was comforted by the unexpected work that he'd received from a certain gentleman from San Francisco, whose lifeless head now rocked back and forth in the box behind him. Far below, a small steamer lay like a beetle on the delicate and brilliant blue that so thickly fills the Bay of Naples; the ship's horn was sounding its final calls, and they echoed cheerfully across the island, where every hillcrest, every contour, every stone was so clearly visible that it seemed there was no air at all. Near the docks, the junior porter saw his senior counterpart race by in an automobile with the dead man's wife and daughter, both of them pale, their eyes sunken from sleeplessness and tears. Ten minutes later the ship left port, stirring the water once more as it headed for Sorrento and Castellammare, and carried the family from San Francisco forever from Capri. . . . Quietude and calm settled on the island in its wake.

Two thousand years ago that island was inhabited by a man who somehow held power over millions of people. He gratified his lust in ways that are repugnant beyond words, and carried out immeasurable atrocities against his subjects. Humanity has remembered him through time, and now countless people come from all around the world to see the ruins of his stone house on one of the island's highest peaks. The tourists who had traveled

to Capri with this aim were still asleep on that lovely morning, although small, mouse-grey donkeys with red saddles were already
being led to the entrances of their hotels, so that all the old and
young American and German guests could clamber up onto
their backs after a big breakfast and a good night's sleep, and
once again old, impoverished women would run behind them
on stone paths with sticks in their sinewy hands, driving those
donkeys all the way to the top of Mount Tiberius. Relieved that
the dead old man from San Francisco—who'd planned to make
this trip with all the others, but wound up only frightening them
with an unpleasant reminder about mortality—had now been
sent away to Naples, the guests slept very soundly; it was quiet on
the island, and everything in town was closed except a small out-
door market on the square, where simple people sold fish and
vegetables, and, as usual, Lorenzo stood without a care. He was a
tall old boatman, an aimless wanderer, and a handsome model,
well known throughout Italy for the many pictures in which he'd
appeared. Having sold for next to nothing a pair of lobsters that
he caught the night before—they were rustling now in the apron
of the cook from the very same hotel where the family from San
Francisco had spent the night—he was free to stand placidly on
that square until the sun went down, smoking a clay pipe and
looking at his surroundings like a king, preening in his shabby
clothes, a red wool beret tugged down over one ear. Meanwhile,
high among the cliffs of Mount Solaro, two Abruzzian mountain
dwellers were following a Phoenician road down from Anacapri,
descending ancient steps cut into the crags. One had a bagpipe
made of a large goatskin and two reeds under his leather cloak;
the other carried an ancient wooden flute. They walked and the
entire country—joyful, lovely, bathed in light—spread out before
them: almost all the island and its stone mounds lay at their feet,

surrounded by a pure, fantastic blue; a mist shimmered over the sea to the east as the hot and blinding sun rose higher and higher; and the azure haze of the Italian mountain mass still wavered in the morning light, the beauty of its near and distant peaks beyond the power of the human word. Halfway down they paused: above the road, in a grotto cut into the mountainside, the meek and gentle Holy Mother stood in pure white plaster robes, her halo flecked with a golden rust from years of rain. Resplendent in the strong, warm light of the sun, she held her eyes toward the sky, toward the eternal, blissful dwelling place of her thrice-blessed child. They took off their hats, and with humble, innocent joy they praised the morning and the sun, praised her, the pure protector of all who suffer in this beautiful and evil world, praised the child born from her womb in a cave in Bethlehem, in a poor shepherd's hut, in the distant land of Judea.

The body of the dead old man from San Francisco was going home, returning to a grave on the shores of the New World. For a week it wandered from one port shed to another, suffering great degradation and neglect, until at last it wound up on the same celebrated ship that had only recently brought it to the Old World with such consideration and regard. But now they hid the gentleman from San Francisco from the living: they lowered him in a tarred coffin deep into the blackness of the ship's hold. And again, again the ship set out on its distant route across the ocean. It sailed past the island of Capri at night, and its lights, slowly disappearing into the dark sea, seemed sad to those who watched from the shore. But the ship's halls were filled with people and the festive glow of chandeliers that night, for as usual a ball was being held.

There was dancing on the second night, and on the third as well—again in the midst of a raging storm, the deep moaning of the sea like a mass for the dead, its black hills fringed with silver foam like the cloaks of passing mourners. The devil could barely see the ship's countless, glowing eyes through the falling snow as he stood on the cliffs of Gibraltar, the stone gate between two worlds, and watched the *Atlantis* sail off into the darkness and the storm. The devil was as huge as a mountainside, but the ship was also huge, with its many stories and its smokestacks—all of it born from the arrogance of the New Man, whose heart is old. The storm tore at its rigging and the wide-mouthed smokestacks as they turned white with snow, but the ship was hard, unyielding, majestic, terrible. At the top of its uppermost story, a comfortable, dimly lit cabin jutted up into the whirling snow, and there the ship's massive driver sat like a pagan idol, reigning over the vessel, alert and anxious in his unremitting somnolence. He could hear the siren's muffled howls and bitter shrieks through the wind, but just beyond the wall of his living quarters, another cabin stood—it seemed to be plated in armor, and it filled again and again with a secret hum, a blue flickering, a dry crackling flame that flared up and burst, illuminating the pale face and the metal headset of the telegraph engineer—and although this room was ultimately an utter mystery to the captain, its close proximity reassured him in the storm. At the very bottom of the *Atlantis*, deep in its underwater belly, twenty-ton cauldrons of steel shone dimly as they rasped with steam, as they dripped boiling water and oil, hulking among various other machines in a kind of kitchen where hellish furnaces heated everything from below and made the ship move: terrifying in its concentration, all the seething force contained within those cauldrons bubbled and surged toward the keel, traveling an endless passageway, a circular, dimly lit tunnel, a gaping maw with its entire length filled by a massive shaft that lay like a monster in an oily bed, slowly and continuously turning with such inexorable regularity that it would wear away the human soul. But in the middle of the ship—in the dining rooms and the ballrooms, everything was filled with joy and light, filled with the murmuring of the well-dressed crowd and the scent of fresh flowers, filled with the songs of the stringed orchestra. And once again, beneath those brilliant chandeliers, among the silks and jewels and the bared flesh of female shoulders, that delicate pair of graceful hired lovers spun and swayed, and ground against each other fitfully, with anguished passion: a sinfully modest young woman with lowered eyes and the hairstyle of an innocent girl, and a strapping young man in a narrow tuxedo with long tails and the most elegant patent leather shoes, his face powdered white, his black hair so perfectly combed it seemed to be glued to his scalp—a beautiful man resembling a giant leech. No one knew that this pair had long ago grown tired of faking their tormented bliss while the shamelessly sad music played on, nor what lay deep, deep below them, in the blackness of the hold, beside the hot, dark innards of the ship as it toiled to overcome the darkness, the sea, the storm.

[1915]

Little Fool

During his vacation, the deacon's son, a seminarian, went to visit his parents in the country. One night he awoke to a sharp stirring in his body, and as he lay in the hot summer dark, his imagination aroused him even more: From behind a willow bush he watches girls go down to the river. It's late afternoon, and they have come from work. They pull their shirts over their heads, and sweat glistens on their white skin. They bend their backs and tip their faces to the sun. They laugh and shout, fling themselves into the blazing water. . . . No longer able to control himself, the seminarian left his bed and stole through the darkened hallway to the kitchen, which was as hot and black as a working oven. With his hands stretched out before him, he groped toward the plank bed where the cook lay sleeping. A destitute girl with no family, she was said to be an imbecile — a little fool—and she was too afraid to scream. The seminarian lived with her all summer, and soon she had a son, who spent his infancy beside his mother in the kitchen. The deacon and the constable and both their wives, the priest himself and his entire household, the shopkeeper's family—all of them knew where the little boy came from, and when the seminarian visited on holidays, he felt such bitter shame he couldn't stand to look upon his past: he'd slept with an imbecile!

After graduation—"A brilliant student," the deacon told everyone—the seminarian returned home for the summer before entering the academy. As soon as they could, his parents invited guests to tea in order to display the future academician. All the guests talked about his brilliant future, drank tea, ate different kinds of jam. The happy deacon wound up the gramophone; it was like a whispering that grew into a shout in the midst of the lively conversations—everyone fell silent and smiled with pleasure at the stirring notes of "On the Road." Suddenly the cook's little boy flew into the room and began a clumsy dance, stomping his feet out of time with the music. His mother had stupidly whispered to him, "Go and dance, my darling," thinking the guests would find it touching. But everyone was shocked by the boy's sudden appearance. The seminarian turned purple with rage, lunged at the child like a tiger, and sent him reeling into the hall.

On his demand, the deacon and the deacon's wife fired the cook the next day. They were kind, compassionate people, and they'd grown used to the cook—they loved her innocence and obedience—so they asked their son to forgive her. But he remained adamant, and they didn't dare disobey. The cook wept quietly as she left the yard that evening, holding a little bundle in one hand and leading her son with the other.

All summer she wandered with him through villages and towns, begging in the name of Christ. She wore out her shoes and her clothes; she was burnt by the sun and the wind; her body turned to skin and bones. But she did not stop. Leaning on a tall staff, she walked barefoot with a sackcloth bag on her shoulder. In the villages and towns she bowed silently before each house. The boy walked beside her with a bag on his shoulder as well; he wore his mother's old shoes, which were broken and stiff—the kind of shoes you'd see lying around in a ditch.

He was a freak. The broad, flat top of his head was covered with a shock of coarse, red hair; his nose lay almost flat on his face; his nostrils were too big; his walnut-colored eyes shone with a strange brilliance. But he was lovely when he smiled.

[1940]

Muza

ALTHOUGH I was well past my youth, I'd gotten it into my head to learn how to paint—I'd loved painting all my life. So I left my estate near Tambov to spend the winter studying in Moscow, where I took lessons from a fairly well-known and utterly talentless artist. A fat, slovenly man, he'd mastered all the requisite artifices: a condescending air, an offhand manner with everyone he met, a velvet coat the color of a pomegranate, and a pair of dirty grey gaiters, which I especially hated. With a pipe in his teeth and his hair combed back in long, greasy curls, he would glance at a student's work, screw up his eyes, and say, as if to himself, "Amusing, most amusing. . . . A sure success."

During those days I lived on the Arbat—in the Capital Hotel, right next to the Prague Restaurant. I worked with the artist or painted in my room during the day, and spent most my evenings with new bohemian friends—some of them were young, others were old and seedy, but they all had the same affection for billiards, crawfish, and beer. How sad and dull it was! The gloomy Capital, that girlish artist and his grimy clothes, his "creatively" neglected studio with dusty props strewn around the floor. Mostly I remember the constant blur of falling snow outside my window, the muffled ring of harness bells and the scrape of horse-drawn trams on the Arbat, the sour smell of beer and gaslights in a hazy restaurant. I don't know why I lived so miserably—I was far from poor.

One day in March I was working in my room. The air drifting through the open *fortochka* was damp from the rain and the wet snow outside, but it was no longer winter air; the sharp clattering of the horses' hooves sounded of spring, and the jingling harness bells seemed almost musical. I was sketching with pastels when someone knocked on the door. "Who is it?" I shouted, but no answer followed. I waited, shouted again, and again heard nothing—then, another knock. I went into the hall and opened the door: on the threshold stood a tall young woman in a grey winter hat, grey overshoes, and a grey coat. She stared straight at me with eyes the color of acorns. Drops of rain and melting snow glistened on her face, her long eyelashes, the hair under the brim of her hat. She looked at me and said:

"I'm Muza Graf—I study in the conservatory. I heard that you're an interesting man, so I came to meet you. Is that all right with you?"

"I'm very flattered," I said, surprised but trying to be polite. "You're welcome anytime. But I should warn you—the rumors that you've heard aren't true: there's nothing interesting about me."

"All the same, why don't you ask me in?" she said, still staring straight into my eyes. "Since I've flattered you, you shouldn't keep me in the hall."

She came inside as if entering her own home, removed her hat, and patted down her chestnut hair before my chipped and greying mirror. Then she slipped off her coat, tossed it over a chair, and sat down on the couch in a checkered flannel dress.

Her nose was wet from the rain and snow. She sniffled. "There's a handkerchief in my coat pocket, bring it to me please," she said commandingly. "And help me with these overshoes."

I brought the handkerchief; she wiped her nose and stretched her legs toward me. "I saw you at Shor's concert yesterday," she said indifferently.

Suppressing a stupid smile of pleasure and surprise—what an eccentric guest!—I timidly removed her overshoes. She smelled of fresh, cold air; the smell excited me. And the boldness that was somehow fused with youth and femininity in her features—in her forthright eyes, in her large and pretty hands—all of it excited me as I removed those overshoes while she sat with her round full knees beneath her dress, and I glimpsed the thin grey stockings stretched across her calves, her narrow feet in patent leather shoes.

Then she settled into the couch, obviously content to stay awhile. Not knowing what to talk about, I started asking questions. Who told her about me? What had she heard? Who was she? Where did she live?

"It doesn't matter where I heard about you. I really came because I saw you at the concert—you're quite handsome. And I live not far from here, on Prechistensky Boulevard; my father's a doctor."

She spoke abruptly, almost sharply.

"Would you like some tea?" I asked, again not knowing what to say.

"I would. And if you have some money, send the bellhop for some apples," she said. "Belov's has Rennets—it's right on the Arbat. But tell him to hurry—I don't like waiting."

"And you seem so easygoing."

"Things are rarely how they seem."

When the bellhop brought the samovar and a bag of apples, she made us tea and wiped the cups and spoons, despite the fact that they were clean. And after eating a Rennet with her tea, she nestled farther into the couch, patted the place beside her, and said, "Now, come sit next to me."

I went to her and she embraced me, kissed my lips unhurriedly, then pulled away and briefly studied my face. As if she'd reassured herself that I was worthy, she closed her eyes and began again—she kissed me for a long time, with a kind of studied, slow precision.

"Well then," she said, as if relieved. "That's all for now. Day after tomorrow."

It had grown completely dark; only the street lamps cast a sad, dim light into the room. You can imagine how I felt. Why this sudden happiness? Why this young, strong woman? The unusual taste . . . the rare shape of her lips. . . . I heard the steady monotone of harness bells and clattering hooves like something from a dream.

"I'd like to have lunch with you at the Prague day after tomorrow," she said. "I've never eaten there—I'm really very inexperienced. I can imagine what you're thinking, but the truth is, you're my first love."

"Love?"

"What would you call this?"

Soon after that I quit my lessons, although she continued taking classes now and then at the conservatory. And instead of parting ways, we lived like newlyweds. We went to galleries and concerts, even sat through public lectures. . . . At her suggestion, I moved in May to an old estate near Moscow—the owners had built dachas on their land and put them up for rent. She took the train to visit me, returning to the city after midnight. I would never have expected such a life—a little summer house near Moscow and days without a thing to do, an estate so different from the one I owned in the steppe, a climate so unlike the one at home.

Evergreens and constant rain. . . . Again and again, white clouds gather in the blue above the trees, the thunder starts to roll, and then a shimmering rain falls through the sunlight, steams in the heat, becomes a mist that smells of pine. And everything's damp; everything's lush, rinsed to a sheen. . . . The pond on the estate resembled a huge black mirror half-buried in the weeds, and the trees were so massive that our dachas looked like little shacks scattered around a forest in the tropics. I lived in a log cabin at the edge of the park. It was still in need of work— they hadn't caulked the walls or planed the floor; the stove didn't have a screen, and most of the rooms lacked furniture. I left a pair of boots under the bed, and soon they were covered in a mold as thick as velvet from the constant damp.

It never grew dark before midnight: among hushed trees the twilight of the west hung on and on. When the moon came out, its still and spellbound light mixed strangely with that lingering dusk. The silence of the forest, the calm air, and the peaceful sky promised an end to the rain as I dozed off in my cabin after walking her to the station, but later I'd be woken by another downpour pelting the roof, more thunderclaps as lightning plumbed the dark. In the morning, the lilac-colored earth was speckled with shade and blinding spots of light; thrushes made a reedy, churring sound, and small birds called flycatchers ticked like metal tapping stone among the leaves. The air turned hot and heavy by midday; clouds bunched up, and soon more rain was coming down. The sky would clear again in the evening, and as the sun set, its rays streamed through the leaves, sloped into my room, formed a golden grid that flashed and wavered on the rough, log-cabin walls like light refracted by a crystal. Then I'd leave to meet her at the station. The arriving train would unload throngs of people headed for their dachas, the smell of burning coal would mix with the damp, fresh air of the forest, and she'd appear among the crowd, holding a string bag, her arms weighed down with fruit and packages of food, a bottle of Madeira. . . . We always dined alone, enjoying each other's company. . . . Before her train back to Moscow, we'd wander in the park, and she'd lean her head on my shoulder like a woman walking in her sleep beside a black pond where ancient trees reach into the stars, where the pale night sky stuns us with its infinite silence, and the shadows of the evergreens fall endlessly across fields that look like silver lakes in the distance.

In June we moved to my estate near Tambov; we didn't marry, but she lived with me and ran the household as if she were my wife. During the long fall she was content to occupy her time with reading and everyday chores. Our most regular visitor from among the neighbors was a lonely, impoverished land-owner named Zavistovsky. He lived only two *versts* away, and during the winter he began coming to our house almost every night. I'd known him since childhood, and I soon grew so used to his presence that it seemed strange to be at home without him. He was a red-haired, frail, timid, and slow-witted man, but he was a fairly good musician. The two of us would play checkers, or Muza and he would play duets on the piano.

Just before Christmas I made a trip into town. The moon was already up when I returned. Entering the house, I failed to find her anywhere.

"Where is your ladyship, Dunya?" I asked the maid while drinking tea alone. "Did she go for a walk?"

"I don't know, sir. She's been gone since breakfast."

"She dressed and left," my old nurse said gloomily as she passed through the dining room without looking up.

"Must have gone to Zavistovsky's," I thought to myself. "They're probably on their way back here, it's already seven." Still chilled from my journey, I lay down in the study and unexpectedly dozed off. And just as suddenly, I snapped out of my sleep an hour later with a clear and savage thought: "She's left me! She's hired a *mouzhik* to take her to the station—gone back to Moscow! She could do anything! But maybe she's here now. . . . Maybe she's come back. . . ." I walked through the house again. "No, not here. . . . And the servants see me searching for her. . . . Humiliating."

At about ten, not knowing what else to do, I put on my coat, picked up my gun for some reason, and left on the main road for Zavistovsky's. "It's as if he didn't come on purpose today—and I have the whole damn night ahead of me! Has she really left me? It's impossible, no!" I walk and my boots squeal in the packed snow of the road. White fields shine to my left under a low, pitiful moon. . . . I turn off the main road and approach the sorry-looking estate: a row of barren trees leading across a field, the entrance to the courtyard, the run-down house standing to the left, all of it in darkness. . . . The porch is covered with ice. I climb the steps and wrench open the door with its tattered padding and upholstery: the foyer glows from the flames of an open stove. It's warm and dark. . . . Even in the living room it's dark. . . .

"Vikenty Vikentich!"

Wearing felt boots, he appeared without a sound at the threshold of his study. There too it was dark, except for the moonlight falling through a three-pane window.

"Oh, it's you. Come in, come in," he said. "I was just sitting here in the twilight, enjoying a night without lamps."

I entered and sat down on his battered couch.

"Can you believe it—Muza's disappeared."

He was silent for a moment. And then, in a voice I could barely hear:

"Yes, I understand you."

"You 'understand'? What do you mean?"

Immediately Muza entered the study from the adjoining bedroom. Like him, she wore felt boots; like him, she moved without a sound, a shawl around her shoulders.

"I see you've brought a gun," she said, sitting down on the couch opposite me. "If you want to shoot, shoot me, not him."

Everything was visible in the golden moonlight coming through the window. I looked at her felt boots and her knees under her grey skirt. I wanted to scream, "I can't live without you—I would die for those knees and that skirt, those boots!"

"Everything's finished," she said. "It's over. There's no point in making a scene."

"You're a monster," I said, choking on the words.

"Could you give me a cigarette, darling?" she said to Zavis-tovsky. He timidly leaned toward her, extended his cigarette case, and began digging in his pockets for a match.

"You already speak to me like a stranger," I gasped. "Couldn't you wait to call him 'darling'?"

"Why?" she asked, raising her eyebrows while the cigarette dangled from her fingers.

My heart hammered in my throat. Blood throbbed in my temples . . . I got up and staggered out.

[1938]

Old Woman

THE OLD WOMAN came from far away to Moscow. She calls her northern region Rus. She's big, round-hipped—wears felt boots and a bulky, quilted vest. Her face is large; her eyes are yellow; her thick grey hair's unkempt—an eighteenth-century character.

Once I asked how old she is.

"I am seventy-seven, sir."

"And god willing, you'll long continue on this earth."

"Why not? Those aren't so many years. My father lived to be a hundred."

She drinks hot water, eats black bread with herring or pickles, never touches tea or sugar.

"You've been healthy all those years, I'm sure."

"No, I had the shaking sickness once. Someone cast a spell

on me. I was terrified of my husband. If he came to me for love, I'd shake and writhe. I'd burn her alive—the one who cast that spell."

The phrase "to burn alive" is among her favorites. She has harsh words for atheists:

"How dare they say such things. God's ours, not theirs. I'd burn them all alive."

Her stories of her homeland are magnificent. The forests there are dark and overgrown. Sometimes the snow piles higher than the tops of the hundred-year-old pines. People sail along the roads in bast sleds towed by shaggy, stocky horses. They wear sheepskin coats dyed sky-blue with tall stiff collars that are made of dog fur, like their hats. The cold burns right through your chest. At dusk the setting sun's like something from a fairy tale, playing on the land with lilac-colored light and bursts of brilliant red, or cloaking everything in green and gold. Stars at night the size of swans' eggs. . . .

[1930]

Rusya

SOMETIME after 10 P.M. the Moscow-Sevastopol express made an unscheduled stop at a small station past Podolsk and stood waiting for something on the other track. A couple riding in first class leaned toward an open window: outside a conductor was crossing the rails with a red lantern swinging from his hand.

"Why have we stopped?" the lady asked abruptly.

The conductor explained that another train that crossed their line was running late: they had to let it pass.

It was already dark and lonely at the station. The sun had set long ago, but in the west, beyond the station and the black, wooded fields, the ghostly light of Moscow's summer dusk remained. Moist air from the marshes drifted through the open windows, and in the silence one could hear the steady, monotonous screech of a corncrake—somehow the sound seemed as damp as the air.

The man propped his elbows up on the window; the woman leaned against his shoulder.

"I stayed here once during summer vacation when I was a student," he said. "I was a tutor at an estate about five *versts* from here. It's a boring place—a sparse forest and a lot of magpies. Mosquitoes. Dragonflies. And no good view of the land. If you really wanted to look at the horizon, you had to go to the house, up to the mezzanine. The house had been built in the fashion of most summer estates, but the family had fallen on hard times, and it was badly run down. Behind it there was something you could call a garden, and beyond that there was something you couldn't call a lake, but couldn't call a swamp either—just a mass of weeds and water lilies, and, of course, a flat-bottomed boat near a marshy shore."

"And, of course, a girl who's dying from boredom at her dacha until you start paddling her around the swamp."

"Yes, everything according to plan. Only the girl wasn't bored at all. And I took her out in the boat at night most of the time. It was really rather poetic. The sky in the west stayed a strange, transparent green all night, and something always seemed to be smoldering on the horizon, just like it is now. . . . I could only find one oar, and it was like a shovel, so I had to paddle like a savage—first on the right side, then on the left. On the other bank it was dark from the forest, but behind the trees that strange half-light glowed all night. And everywhere it's unbelievably quiet—only the mosquitoes whine and the dragonflies buzz past. I never thought they flew at night, but it turns out they do for some reason. The noise they make is downright frightening."

They finally heard the other train rumbling toward them. A breeze rose as it flew by, and the lights in the passing cars blended into a long, golden streak. Then the express lurched forward; an attendant entered the couple's compartment, turned on the lights, and began making their beds.

"So what happened with you and that girl? A full-scale affair? For some reason you've never mentioned her before. What was she like?"

"Skinny. Tall. She wore a yellow sarafan. It was made of cotton, sleeveless. And peasant shoes that had been woven from different colored wools."

"One of those girls who likes a very 'Russian' style. . . ."

"I think it was more a poor woman's style. She never had anything to wear other than that dress. She was an artist—studied painting at the Stroganov School for fine arts. And she looked like something from a painting, from an icon even—a braid of black hair down her back; a dark face with a few freckles; a straight, thin nose. Her eyes and eyebrows were black. . . . And her hair was thick and dry, slightly curly. Her features and her skin looked very beautiful against the yellow cotton and the white muslin sleeves of her shirt. I remember how her ankles and the tops of her feet always seemed very fragile. The skin over them was so delicate you could see her bones."

"I know that type. I had a girlfriend at the university like that. Very prone to hysterics, right?"

"Maybe. Her face was a lot like her mother's, and her mother suffered from terrible depression. She was some kind of princess by birth, had Eastern blood. She'd only come out of her room for meals. She'd come out, sit down—and dead silence. Maybe she'd cough, but she'd never look up from her plate—just shift her knife and fork around from one place to another. And if she did suddenly say something, she'd shout out her words and we'd all jump."

"And the father?"

"He was pretty silent too. Very tall and very removed—a retired military man. But their son was sweet—he's who I tutored."

The attendant said their beds were ready, wished them good night, and left the compartment.

"And what was her name?"

"Rusya."

"What kind of name is that?"

"Very simple—short for Marusya."

"And so, you were really in love with her?"

"Terribly in love. At least that's how it seemed at the time."

"And she?"

He fell silent for a moment, then answered dryly: "She probably thought the same thing. But let's go to bed—I'm exhausted."

"Oh, very nice! You've just gotten me interested! Come on—tell me in two words how the romance ended."

"It ended in nothing. I left and it was over."

"And why didn't you marry her?"

"Evidently I had a premonition that I'd meet you."

"No, really?"

"No. Actually, I shot myself, and she stabbed herself with a dagger."

Having washed their faces and brushed their teeth, the man and the woman locked themselves into the compartment, which seemed to grow more cluttered in the dark, and lay down on their beds, feeling that joy all travelers experience when they finally touch fresh linen sheets and rest their heads on those lustrous pillows that always slip down from the slightly raised end of the berth.

A blue night-light glowed above the door, as if quietly watching over the cabin. She quickly dozed off, but he was unable to sleep and lay smoking in bed, returning to that summer in his thoughts.

She had small, dark freckles on her stomach and her back as well—and they delighted him. Because she wore soft shoes without heels, her whole body seemed to sway under the yellow sarafan when she walked. The sarafan was light and loose-fitting, and her tall, girlish body moved freely under it. Once, her feet soaked by the rain, she ran from the garden into the living room: he hurried to remove her shoes, kissed the narrow, wet soles of her feet—and there had never been such happiness in his life. Everyone had gone to sleep in the darkened house after lunch; more and more fresh-smelling rain was pouring over the patio beyond the open doors—and how terribly that rooster frightened them as he too ran from the garden into the living room, his black feathers shot with a strange, metallic green, his crown as brilliant as a flame, his claws clicking on the floor at the very moment when they'd lost themselves and let all caution go. Seeing how they jumped up from the couch, he ducked his head, as if embarrassed, and politely trotted back into the rain with his shimmering tail drawn down.

In the beginning she'd scrutinized him constantly; if he spoke, she'd blush darkly and mutter something droll. At meals she liked to tease him, saying loudly to her father: "Don't give him any, papa. It's useless. He doesn't like *vareniki*. He doesn't like *okroshka* or noodles, either. He despises yogurt too, and he hates cottage cheese."

He was busy with his pupil in the mornings, and she had

chores to do—the entire household depended on her. They'd have lunch at one, and then she'd go to her room on the mezzanine or, if it wasn't raining, to the garden, where she'd paint the landscape, waving off mosquitoes as she stood before her easel under the birches. Then she began to come out on the balcony, where he usually sat reading in a wicker chair after lunch. She'd stand with her hands behind her back and look at him with a vague smile.

"Can I ask what subtleties you're absorbed in today?"

"The history of the French Revolution."

"Oh my! I didn't realize that we have a revolutionary in the house!"

"Why aren't you painting?"

"My lack of talent is becoming too obvious. I'm about to quit for good."

"Why don't you show me one of your pictures?"

"Why? Do you think you know something about painting?"

"You're awfully proud, you know."

"Yes, that is a flaw of mine."

One day she finally suggested that they take the boat out on the lake. "It looks like the rainy season has ended in this little jungle of ours," she said decisively. "Let's play while we have the chance. Of course, our boat is rotting and it's full of holes, but Petya and I have stopped the floor with marsh weeds."

It was a stifling afternoon. Hot, damp air had settled like a sheet on the grass flecked with buttercups along the shore; pale green moths hovered lazily above the flowers. As they walked to the boat, he began to speak in the same mocking tone that she'd adopted so consistently with him:

"You've finally come down from your pedestal to visit me!"

"And you've finally figured out a way to talk to me," she answered happily as she jumped into the bow, and startled frogs splashed into the water all around them. Suddenly she screamed, pulled the sarafan above her knees, and started stamping: "A snake! A snake!"

He glimpsed the wet, dark skin of her calves as he grabbed the oar from the bow; then he struck the grass snake coiled in the bottom of the boat and flung it far out into the lake.

She had turned pale with a kind of Indian pallor, and the contrast made her freckles seem darker, her hair and eyes even blacker.

"How disgusting!" she said. "It's no wonder the devil took the form of a snake. They're everywhere around here—in the garden, under the house. And Petya picks them up with his hands! Can you believe it!"

It was the first time she'd spoken to him openly; the first time they'd looked straight into each other's eyes.

"But you were quick! You hit him perfectly!"

Relaxed again, she smiled as she scampered from the bow and sat down in the stern. The beauty she'd revealed in her terror stunned him. "She's still a little girl," he thought with tenderness. But he tried to appear nonchalant as he stepped carefully into the boat, stuck his oar into the gelatinous bottom of the lake, swung the bow forward, and began to pole through the tangled weeds, the tufts of marsh grass, and the blooming lilies that layered the surface with their broad, flat leaves. When they finally reached open water, he sat down on the seat in the middle of the boat and began rowing—first on the right, then on the left.

"This is nice, isn't it?" she shouted.

"Yes, very nice!" he answered, taking off his cap and turning toward her. "Would you mind keeping this near you? I'm afraid I'll knock it into the bottom of this wreck—it's full of leeches, you know, and it still leaks."

She put the cap on her knees.

"Don't worry about it—just put it somewhere dry up there."

She hugged the hat against her chest: "No—I'm going to guard it!"

Tenderness welled up in his heart again, but he turned away and started rowing harder in the water that shimmered between the lilies and the weeds.

Mosquitoes began to bite his hands and face, and the silver glare of the lake was blinding. . . . Humid air and a shifting band of sunlight. . . . Thin white strands of clouds shining in the sky and on the water glades among the leafy islands. . . . It was shallow everywhere, and he could see marsh grass growing on the bottom of the lake, but the water's depth seemed endless when the sky and the clouds' reflections stretched across it. Suddenly she screamed again, and they began to tip: she had reached down from the stern toward a lily, grabbed its stem, and pulled so hard that the boat heaved to one side and she began to fall—he barely had time to catch her under her arms. She burst out laughing, fell into the bow, and flicked the water from her hand into his eyes. Then he grabbed her again and suddenly, without knowing what he was doing, he kissed her lips as she laughed. She put her arms around his neck and clumsily kissed his cheek.

From that time on, they started boating on the lake at night.

The next day she called him into the garden after lunch.

"Do you love me?" she asked.

Remembering the way they'd kissed in the boat, he answered earnestly: "From the first day we met."

"And I," she said, "—no, I hated you at first because you

never seemed to notice me. But that's over now, thank God. When everyone goes to bed tonight, go down to the lake and wait for me. Only be careful—sneak out quietly. Mama watches everything I do—she's insanely jealous."

That night she came to the shore carrying a blanket.

"What's that for?" he asked, flustered by the joy he felt at seeing her.

"You're so silly—we're bound to get cold. Let's hurry—get in and row us over to the other shore."

They crossed the lake without speaking.

"Okay, that's good," she said as the boat neared the forest on the other bank. "Now come here. Where's the blanket? Oh, I'm sitting on it. Wrap it around me—I'm freezing. And sit here. No, you see, we didn't kiss right yesterday. Now I'll kiss you first, only very, very softly. And you put your arms around me. . . . Everywhere. . . ."

Under the sarafan she was wearing only a camisole. Tenderly, barely touching him, she kissed the edges of his lips. He felt as if his head were spinning as he pushed her back into the stern, and she pressed herself against him. . . .

Afterward they lay resting quietly in the boat. Then she sat up and smiled in a way that expressed both happy exhaustion and lingering pain.

"Now we're husband and wife," she said. "Mama says she won't survive it if I get married, but I don't want to think about that now. . . . You know what? I'm going swimming. I love to at night."

Her long, thin body looked pale in the gloom when she pulled off her dress and began to wrap her braid around her head, exposing her underarms and making her breasts rise as she reached up: she was not at all embarrassed by her nakedness or the dark hair below her belly. Finished with her braid, she kissed him lightly, jumped onto her feet, and splashed into the lake. Holding her head out of the water, she kicked loudly as she swam.

Then he hurriedly helped her dress and wrapped her up in the blanket. Her eyes and her black hair, still tied in a braid, stood out sharply in the dim light. He didn't dare to touch her anymore; he only kissed her hands and sat without talking, seized by an almost unbearable joy. Sometimes they heard a light rustling in the leaves, and it seemed that someone was standing among the black trees and the scattered lights of the fireflies on the bank—standing and listening to them. She raised her head: "Wait, what was that?"

"Don't worry, it's probably a frog going up the bank. Or a hedgehog in the woods."

"But what if it's a goat."

"What goat?"

"I don't know. But just imagine it: a goat comes out of the forest and stands there and watches us. . . . Oh, I'm so happy I just feel like saying stupid things!"

He pressed her hands to his lips again, then solemnly kissed her cold, damp breast. How suddenly she'd changed, become a wholly different creature in his eyes! The green summer twilight had not gone out; it was still glowing beyond the darkened forest, still hanging on the calm, pale surface of the lake. A sharp scent like the smell of celery rose from the dew-soaked weeds along the bank; the whining sound of the mosquitoes turned tentative, almost pleading—and terrifying, sleepless dragonflies darted over the water and the boat with their delicate, crackling wings. And still, still something rustled in the leaves, crawled, picked its way carefully among the roots. . . .

A week later he was disgraced, thrown out of the house, and forbidden to see her again. The scandal and their sudden, violent separation left him stunned.

They had been sitting in the living room after lunch, their heads lightly touching as they looked at the pictures in an old issue of *Niva*.

"Do you still love me?" he asked, pretending to study the drawings.

"Silly, you're so silly," she whispered.

Suddenly they heard someone running lightly toward the room, and her half-mad mother appeared at the threshold in a tattered black silk dressing gown and worn-out leather slippers. She rushed at them like an actress making her entrance on stage, her black eyes flashing with a tragic light.

"I know everything! I felt it! I've been watching you! I won't let you take her, you bastard!"

She flung up her hand and fired a deafening shot from the ancient pistol that Petya used to frighten sparrows—there was only powder in the gun. He jumped at her through the smoke and grabbed her arm, but she wrenched free and struck his forehead with the pistol. Then she threw the gun at him and started shouting even more theatrically as blood trickled down his face and others in the house ran toward the noise.

"You'll have to step over my dead body to leave this house with her!" she screamed, her lips flecked with foam. "I'll hang myself the day you take her! Do you hear—I'll hang myself! I'll throw myself off the roof! Get out, you bastard—get out of my house! You choose, Marya Viktorovna—choose! Him or your mother!"

"You, mama," she whispered, "you. . . ."

He came back to himself and opened his eyes—the blue

night-light above the door was still staring at him with morbid curiosity in the darkness, and the car was still rocking gently on its springs as the train flew inexorably forward. Already that sad little stop was far away, far back in the distance. And twenty years had passed since he first saw those thickets of trees, those magpies and the swamp, the lilies and the grass snakes and the cranes. . . . Yes, there were cranes—how could he have forgotten them! Like so much of that summer, they were a mystery, that pair that appeared occasionally on the banks of the swamp and allowed only her to approach them, bending their long, delicate necks and watching with curiosity and suspicion as softly she moved closer in her woven shoes, and finally sat before them, her yellow sarafan spreading out over the wet, warm grass: with childlike wonder she would study their eyes, look into the menacing and beautiful blackness of those pupils ringed by dark grey irises. Watching her and the cranes through binoculars, he could clearly see the birds' small, brilliant heads, the delicate slits of their nares, and the bony, powerful beaks with which they killed grass snakes in one blow. The feathers that thickly covered their torsos and their airy tails glinted like steel, and their legs—one pair black, the other green—resembled long, scaly reeds. Sometimes each bird would stand on just one leg, remaining inexplicably still for hours; then, for no apparent reason, they'd begin to hop and stretch their massive wings, or bob their heads and take slow, measured steps with an air of self-importance, clutching their feet into tight balls as they lifted them, then spreading them apart like a raptor's talons in the air. But still, when she ran toward those cranes, he thought of nothing—saw nothing—but her yellow sarafan spreading out over the grass; and the thought of her dark body—the dark freckles on her skin beneath that sarafan—filled him with such mortal longing that he shuddered.

On that last day, during the last moments in which they sat together on the living room couch with an old copy of *Niva*, she was holding his cap again, and she hugged it against her chest, just as she had in the boat. Her black eyes were shining with joy when she said, "I love you so much that nothing's dearer to me now than the smell of this hat—the smell of your hair and your hideous cologne!"

He was drinking coffee and cognac in the dining car after breakfast as the train rolled on somewhere past Kursk.

"Why are you drinking so much?" his wife asked. "That's already your fifth, isn't it? Are you still sad? Still pining for your dacha girl with bony feet?"

"Still sad, still sad," he answered with an unpleasant smile. "The dacha girl. . . . *Amata nobis quantum amabitur nulla!*"

"Is that Latin? What does it mean?"

"You don't need to know."

"You're so rude," she said as she sighed and began staring out the sunlit window.

[1940]

Old and Young

Lovely summer days and the Black Sea's calm.

A steamer overloaded with people and goods; its deck packed solid from forecastle to stern.

And a long, circular route from the Crimea to the Caucasus, the shores of Anatolia, Constantinople.

Hot sun and blue sky, a lilac-colored sea. Endless stops in crowded ports where the winches crash like thunder and the deckhands shout and curse. *Heave to! Lift!* And then the calm again. A slow and peaceful passage along the base of distant mountains, their peaks melting in the sun's haze.

A cool breeze blows through the spacious, clean, and empty lounge for first-class passengers. But it's dirty and crowded on deck, where throngs of passengers ride in the galley's stench and the engine's heat, sleeping on plank beds under the ship's awnings, or nestled among anchor chains and hawsers on the forecastle. Here there is always a pungent odor: sometimes it's hot and pleasant, sometimes it's warm and disgusting, but always it is stirring—the unmistakable smell of a steamer mixed with the sea's freshness. And here there are hordes of every nationality—Russians and Ukrainians, Athonian Monks, Georgians, Kurds, and Greeks. . . . The Kurds sleep from morning until night, a completely savage race, while the Georgians either sing or dance in pairs: tossing their wide sleeves back with coquettish nonchalance, jumping lightly, and floating into the parting crowd as they clap their hands in rhythm: *tash-tash, tash-tash.* . . . Meanwhile, the Russian pilgrims bound for Palestine never stop drinking tea, and a woman camped near the kitchen watches intently as a slope-shouldered *mouzhik* with straight hair and a narrow yellow beard reads out loud from the Holy Scripture: alone and unabashed, she wears a red jacket and a gauzy green scarf in her lusterless black hair—and her defiant eyes are always fixed on this man as he reads.

I went ashore at Trabzon, where we were docked for a long time. Returning to the ship, I saw a new band of armed and ragged Kurds walking up the gangway—a retinue escorting an elder. Big and broad-chested, he wore an astrakhan and a grey Circassian coat snugly fastened around his narrow waist by a silver-plated belt. All the Kurds already camped on deck—they had gathered there en masse—got up and cleared a space for the newcomer. His retinue put down many rugs and pillows, and then the old man lay down majestically. His beard was white as steam; his face was dark and worn from the sun, and his brown eyes shone with an unusual brilliance.

I walked over to him, crouched, and said, *"Salaam."* Then I asked in Russian if he was coming from the Caucasus.

"From farther away than that, sir," he answered amicably in Russian. "We are Kurds."

"And where are you traveling to?"

"To Istanbul, sir," he answered with modest pride. "To the Padishah himself. I am taking him a gift—seven whips. The Padishah took seven sons from me in the war—all I had. And all seven were killed. Seven times the Padishah brought glory to my name."

"Tsk, tsk, tsk," muttered a young Kerchen Greek with offhanded pity. He was standing above us holding a cigarette—a portly, handsome fop in a cherry-red fez, a grey frock coat and a white vest, stylish slacks, shiny boots that buttoned down the side. "Such an old man to wind up all alone," he said, shaking his head.

The Kurd looked at his fez. "How foolish you are," he answered simply. "It is you who will be old. I'm not old now, and never will be. Do you know about the ape?"

"What ape?" the fop answered uneasily.

"Listen, God made heaven and earth—you know that, right?"

"Well, yes."

"Then God made man. And he said, 'You, man, will live thirty years on the earth. It will be a good life. You will be happy. You will think that everything on earth was made for you alone by God. Are you satisfied with that?' And man thought, 'It's good—but only thirty years to live? That's not enough!' Are you listening?" the old man asked with a sardonic smile.

"I can hear you," the fop responded.

"Then God made a mule and said, 'You, mule, will live thirty years on this earth. You will carry wine sacks and heavy loads. People will ride on your back and beat you over the head with a stick. Are you satisfied with thirty years?' The mule cried out and wept and said to God: 'Why must I live so long? Let me live only fifteen years.' 'And give me fifteen more,' man said to God. 'Please, take fifteen years from his share and give them to me.' And God did as he was asked: Man received forty-five years of life. Things worked out well for man, didn't they?" the old man asked, glancing at the fop.

"Not bad," he answered tentatively, unsure of where all this would lead.

"Then God made a dog and gave him thirty years as well. 'You,' God said to the dog, 'will be angry all your life. You will guard your owner's riches, distrust strangers, stand barking in a doorway. You will not sleep at night for worrying.' And the dog began to howl: 'Please, please—give me only half of such a life.' And again man begged from God: 'Give me his half-life as well!' And again God did as he was asked. How many years does man have now?"

"That would make sixty," the fop answered more happily.

"Well, then God made an ape. He gave him thirty years to live, and said: 'You will live without labor and without concerns. But your face will be unpleasant. It will be bald and wrinkled, and you'll have no eyebrows. You will ask people to look at you, and they will only laugh at your face.'"

"So the ape refused—asked for half as many years as well?" asked the fop.

"That's right, the ape also refused half of his life," the old man answered, sitting up to take the mouthpiece of a water pipe from the Kurd next to him. "And man asked for that half-life as well," he said, lying down again and drawing on the pipe. He fell silent then, and stared straight ahead, as if he had forgotten us. When he began to talk again, he seemed to be addressing no one in particular:

"Man lived his own thirty years like a man—he ate, drank, fought wars, danced at weddings. Loved young women and girls. And for fifteen years he worked like a mule, gathering his riches. For fifteen years he guarded those riches like a dog, barking and being angry, and not sleeping at night. Then he became as old and foul as the ape. And everyone shook their heads and laughed at his old age. And it will all be the same with you," the old man said derisively, rolling the pipe's mouthpiece on his teeth.

"Why hasn't that happened to you?" asked the fop.

"It isn't that way with me."

"But *why*?"

"There are not many people like me," the old man said firmly. "I didn't live like a donkey or a dog. Why now should I live like an ape? Why should I be old?"

[1936]

Styopa

JUST BEFORE evening, the young merchant Krasilshchikov
was caught in a thunderstorm on the road to Chern.

He drove hard in the downpour, sitting high over the front
axle of his light-running *droshky*, the collar turned up on his
long, cloth coat, his feet in big boots planted firmly over the
mudguard. Water streamed from the peaked cap he wore low
over his eyes, and his hands grew cold as he held the slick leather
reins and needlessly urged on the already excited horse. Its
tongue lolling from its mouth, a brown pointer ran in a fountain
of mud that sprayed from the left front wheel.

At first Krasilshchikov followed a black dirt lane near the
highway, but the lane soon turned into a grey, bubbling stream,
and he moved onto the main road, clattering over its surface of
crushed stone. For sometime it had been impossible to see the

surrounding fields and the sky in the showering rain, which smelled of phosphorous and fresh cucumbers. Like a banner repeatedly unfurled to announce the end of the world, lightning burst with a blinding, ruby flash across the entire length of the great cloud wall before him, branching out and twisting into sharp strands as the tail of each bolt sizzled overhead, then exploded in a stunning clap of thunder. The horse flattened its ears and lunged forward with each blast; the dog broke into a leaping stride. . . . Krasilshchikov had grown up and studied in Moscow, but during summers at his Tula estate, which resembled an expensive dacha, he enjoyed his position as a merchant-landowner, a *mouzhik* who'd risen from the peasantry. So he drank Lafitte and carried his cigarettes in a gold-plated case while wearing tarred boots, shirts with collars that button on the side, and the snug-fitting jackets popular among simple country people. He was proud of his healthy Russian build and now, in the thundering downpour, with cold rain streaming from his nose and hat, he felt flush with the energetic joy of country living. That summer he often remembered the previous one, which he'd spent being miserable in Moscow because of an affair he was having with a well-known actress. He'd lingered in the city until July, waiting for her to leave for Kislovodsk: idle days and heat; the stench of green smoke from boiling tar in metal tubs along the dug-up streets; breakfast at the Troitsky café with actors from the Maly Theatre who were also going south to Kislovodsk, empty hours over coffee at Trambler's—and those nights he waited for her in his apartment with the furniture already covered in dust cloths, the chandeliers and the pictures wrapped in muslin, the smell of naphthalene in every room. Moscow evenings are endless in the summer—darkness comes only around eleven; and so he sits and sits—and for hours she isn't there. Then, finally, the bell—she appears in all her summer elegance, says all at once in her breathless voice, "I'm sorry I'm so late. I've been in bed all day with an absolutely brutal headache—yes, your tea rose is terribly faded today. I took the fastest cab I could. I haven't eaten all day—I'm starving."

As the rain and thunderclaps receded, the fields came back into view, and to the left of the highway he saw a familiar two-room hut built from unplaned logs: it was owned by the old widower Pronin, who used one of the rooms as lodging for travelers. Krasilshchikov was still twenty *versts* from town, his horse was already in a lather, and lightning continued to flash across the black sky ahead. "I'll have to stop and wait a little," he decided. At the crossing he turned sharply and pulled up to the inn's small wooden porch.

"Hello! Hey!" he shouted. "You have a guest, old man."

But all the windows under the rusty tin roof were dark; no one answered his call. He wrapped the reins around the *droshky's* front panel and followed his dripping, grimy dog onto the porch. Its eyes shining with a bright, senseless light, the animal looked almost rabid. Krasilshchikov's forehead was damp with sweat; he took off his cap and tossed his waterlogged coat over the porch rail, revealing a tight-fitting jacket and a silver-plated belt. Then he wiped his mud-spattered face and began scraping the muck from his boots with his whip handle. The front door stood open to a small corridor that joined the owner's quarters with the guest room, but the entire building seemed to be deserted. "Must have gone to get the cattle in," he thought as he turned and looked at the field, wondering if he shouldn't drive farther. The evening air was damp and still; in the distance he could hear quail calling cheerfully from the sopped rye. The rain had stopped, but night was coming on; the sky and the land were turning dark and gloomy, and beyond the highway, beyond the ink-black ridge of the forest, the clouds looked even thicker than before, and the lightning still flickered like a red, menacing flame. Krasil-shchikov stepped into the narrow entrance hall and groped through the darkness to the guest room—it too was dark and silent: a cheap clock ticked on the wall. He slammed the door and turned to the left, groping again in the blackness until he found the door that led into the owner's private room: again, there was no one; flies droned on the ceiling as if dissatisfied and half asleep in the hot dark.

"Like they're dead and gone!" Krasilshchikov said out loud, and immediately he heard a soft, hurried voice. Styopa, the innkeeper's daughter, had climbed down from the plank bed in the dark.

"Is that you Vasil Likseich? I'm here all alone. The cook had a big fight with papa and went home, and now papa's taken his helper to town on an errand. They probably won't get back till tomorrow. The storm scared me to death, and all of a sudden I hear someone drive up: it scared me even more. . . . Excuse me, please—hello."

Krasilshchikov struck a match and held it toward her, re-vealing her small, dark-skinned face and black eyes.

"Hello, my little fool," he said. "I was going to town too, but I decided to wait out the storm. . . . And you thought it was thieves pulling in?"

The match began to burn down, but he could still see her smile and her startled expression, the coral necklace she wore, her small breasts under a yellow chintz dress. Slightly more than half his height, she looked exactly like a little girl.

"We need some light," she said hurriedly. Flustered by Krasilshchikov's impertinent stare, she rushed toward the lamp that hung over the table. "God himself must have sent you. What would I do all alone?" she said in her sweet-sounding voice as she stood on her toes and awkwardly lifted the lamp's glass cylinder from its serrated tin base.

Krasilshchikov lit another match and stared at her body as she stretched and leaned away from him. "It's fine like this," he said suddenly, throwing down the match and reaching around her waist. "Wait a minute. Turn around."

She looked at him over her shoulder with frightened eyes, dropped her hands by her sides and turned. He pulled her toward him; she threw her head back in alarm but didn't try to wrench free.

Looking down through the darkness, he fixed his eyes on hers and laughed. "Are you even more frightened now?"

"Vasil Likseich . . . ," she said imploringly as she pulled against his arms.

"Wait, don't you like me? You're always glad when I stop by."

"There's no one on earth better than you," she whispered ardently.

"There—you see." He kissed her lips slowly and his hands slipped farther down.

"Vasil Likseich . . . in the name of Christ. . . . You forgot your horse, it's still by the porch. . . . Papa will come back. . . . No. . . . No, you shouldn't."

Half an hour later he came outside, tied his horse under an awning in the courtyard, took off its bridle, gave it some wet, fresh-cut grass from a hayrack that stood nearby. Then he walked back to the hut, looking up at the peaceful stars and the rain-washed sky. Distant summer lightning still flickered in the hot, dark, and silent room. She was curled up tightly on the plank bed with her chin pressed to her chest, wrung out from crying in ecstasy, shock, and horror at everything that had taken place. He kissed her wet, salty cheek, lay down on his back, and drew her head to his shoulder with his left hand while holding a cigarette in the other. She lay peaceful and silent beside him, her hair lightly touching his chin as he gently stroked it and smoked, his mind wandering. Soon she was fast asleep. He stared up at the darkness and grinned with satisfaction. "Papa went to town." There he goes, and—*voilà*—here we are! It's too bad, though—one look at her and he'll know everything. That withered old man with a little grey coat is shrewd. You can tell by just looking at him—that beard that's white as snow, those black eyebrows of his. He talks nonstop when he's drunk, but his eyes are sharp, and he sees through everyone. . . .

He lay without sleeping until the hut's darkness diminished and the room began to reappear. Turning his head, he saw the greenish hue of the eastern sky turning white outside the window, and in a gloomy corner of the room he noticed a large icon hanging over a table: a saint in holy vestments raised his hand in blessing, an adamant and stern expression on his face. Krasilshchikov looked at the girl: she was still curled up, her knees drawn to her chest, everything forgotten in sleep! A sweet and pitiful girl. . . .

When the sky was completely light and the rooster began to crow in changing tones beyond the wall, he made a move to get out of bed, and she immediately sat up. With her dress unbuttoned and her hair disheveled, she leaned to one side and stared at him with uncomprehending eyes.

"Styopa," he said cautiously. "It's time—I have to go."

"You're already leaving?" she whispered without understanding.

But then she suddenly came to her senses: her fists struck her shoulders as she clasped her arms to her chest. "Where are you going? What will I do without you? What am I supposed to do now?"

"Styopa, I'll come back soon."

"You know papa will be here! How will I see you? I'd come through the woods, but how will I get out of the house?"

He clenched his teeth and pushed her down on her back. She threw out her arms and gasped, as if despairing before death: "Ah!"

And then he was standing in front of the plank bed, already in his tight-fitting jacket and his peaked cap, already holding his whip in his hand. His back was turned to the heavy, brilliant light of the rising sun as she kneeled on the bed, sobbing like a child and contorting her mouth as she struggled to speak:

"Vasil Likseich . . . in the name of Christ. . . . In the name of the heavenly father himself, marry me! I'll be like your slave! I'll sleep by your door! I'd run away with you now if I could, but they'll never let me go. Vasil Likseich. . . ."

"Be quiet," Krasilshchikov said sternly. "In a few days I'll go to your father and tell him that I'm marrying you. Hear?"

She sat back and stopped sobbing, lifted her wet, radiant eyes with a trusting expression. "Really?"

"Of course—really."

"I turned fifteen at Epiphany," she said hurriedly.

"Well, there—you see. Six months and we can marry. . . ."

As soon as he got home he began packing his things; toward evening he drove in his troika to the railway station. Two days later he was already in Kislovodsk.

[1938]

On One Familiar Street

I WAS WALKING in the twilight that fresh, green leaves create when street lamps glow metallically beneath them. It was a spring night in Paris; I felt young and easy with myself, thinking,

> *I remember one familiar street—*
> *One old house, its staircase steep and dark,*
> *A window with the curtain closed. . . .*

A wonderful poem! And how strange it is that I once lived those things. Moscow, Presnya—streets muffled by snow, a wooden, bourgeois little house—and I, a student, some kind of "I" immersed in a life that seems pure fiction now. . . .

A secret lamp still burning late at night . . .

And there too—there was a light. Snow blew down like chalk dust from the roof; like smoke it was dispersed by the wind—and overhead, in the mezzanine, a light burned behind a red, calico curtain. . . .

> *She was beyond all words—the girl who waited*
> *In that house, and met me at a secret hour*
> *With her long hair already down. . . .*

It was just the same. . . . A deacon's daughter. A girl who left her abject family in Serpukhov, came to study in Moscow. . . . And there I was: I went up to the wooden, snow-covered porch, pulled on the ring attached to a long, rustling wire that led into the vestibule—pulled until the bell clapped, and I could hear someone running down the steep wooden stairs: the door flew open, and she was there in the wind, snow blowing across her shawl and her white blouse. I rushed to kiss her, to shelter her from the wind, and we ran up through the freezing darkness of that stairwell to her room, where the air was just as cold and the light from the kerosene lamp was dull. A red curtain on the window, a lamp on a little table, a bed with an iron frame against the wall. . . . I dropped my coat and hat, sat down on the bed, pulled her into my lap. I could feel her body and its small, delicate bones through her skirt. . . . There was no "long hair already down"—only a simple braid of rather plain, light brown hair, and the face of a common girl that hunger had made translucent, only the translucent eyes of a peasant and those tender lips one finds among weak girls.

No longer like a child, she pressed her mouth
To mine. And later, trembling, she whispered
"Together, you and I, we'll run away. . . ."

We'll run away! Where to, for what, from whom? How charming it is—the earnest foolishness of children. There was no running away for us. There was the sweetness of those lips, a sweetness unknown in the rest of the world; there were tears that welled up in our eyes from too much happiness; there was a kind of exhaustion that settled like a weight on our young bodies and made us rest our heads on each other's shoulders—and her lips turning warm, as if she had a fever, as I unbuttoned her blouse, kissed her girlish breasts, their tips like wild, unripe straw-berries. . . . Returning to her senses, she jumped up from the bed, lit a spirit lamp, warmed our weak tea—and we drank it with white bread and red-rind cheese, talking endlessly about our future and feeling the fresh, cold air of winter that streamed from behind the curtain while dry snow ticked against the window pane. "I remember one familiar street. . . ." What else do I remember? I remember how I went with her to Kursk station in the spring, how we hurried on the platform with her willow basket and her red blanket tied in a little bundle, fastened with a belt; I remember how we ran down the long chain of green cars, glancing at the crowds in the packed compartments as the train prepared to leave. . . . I remember how she finally climbed into the corridor of one of those cars, how we kissed each other's hands as we said goodbye, how I promised to go to her in Serpukhov in two weeks' time. . . . I remember nothing more. There was nothing more.

[1944]

Antigone

IN JUNE a student left his mother's estate to visit his aunt and uncle, a general who'd lost his legs. It was important to see how they were getting along and to check on his uncle's health. The student carried out this obligation every summer, and now he felt peacefully resigned to the trip as he sat with one muscular thigh draped over the armrest of the seat in a second-class compartment and read a few pages of a new book by Averchenko, or idly watched the telegraph poles rise and dip down, their white ceramic housings shaped like lilies of the valley. Although he wore a student's white hat with a blue band, he resembled a young officer, for all his clothes and finery had a military style—a white, high-collared jacket, greenish riding pants and shiny leather boots, a cigarette case with a brilliant orange braid.

His aunt and uncle were rich. When he came home from

Moscow, his parents always sent a worker with two draft horses and a heavy *tarantass* instead of a driver with a carriage to meet him, but at the station near his aunt and uncle's house, the student seemed to enter a wealthy stranger's life. He immediately felt strong and happy, handsome, highly refined. And so it was this trip: three spirited bays pulled the light, rubber-wheeled carriage that came to meet him. The young driver wore a sleeveless, dark blue coat over a shirt of yellow silk, and the student took his seat with unwitting, foppish affectation.

Fifteen minutes later the carriage breezed into the driveway of an imposing estate. Its wheels hissed over the sand near a flower bed, and the harness bells rang playfully as the horses rounded the courtyard, then stopped before a new, two-story house. A brawny servant in sideburns came outside to unload the luggage; he wore low-cut boots and a red waistcoat with black stripes. The student made an improbably long and graceful leap from the carriage as his aunt came smiling and swaying to the vestibule door, a big silk chemise draped over her formless body. The flesh sagged on her large face, her nose was shaped like an anchor, and little pouches of yellowing skin hung under her brown eyes. She pecked his cheeks, and he pretended he was glad to see her as he bowed to kiss her warm, dark hand, thinking *three whole days of boredom and lies!* Answering with feigned respect the questions that she asked with feigned concern about his mother, the student followed his aunt into the vestibule and looked with gleeful contempt at the stuffed, slightly hunch-backed bear that stood awkwardly on its hind legs near the stairs, its glass eyes polished to a sheen, a bronze tray for visitors' cards gently cradled in its huge clawed paws. But suddenly he stopped, surprised and overjoyed: the fleshy, pale and blue-eyed general was being wheeled toward him by a beautiful woman in a grey gingham dress with a white apron, a white kerchief covering her hair. Her large grey eyes were radiant with youth and vigor, her delicate hands seemed to shine, and her face was suffused with a fresh, clear light. As he bent to kiss his uncle's hand, the student glanced at her legs and the long, graceful lines of her figure.

"This is my Antigone," the general joked. "Although I'm not as blind as Oedipus—especially when it comes to beautiful women. Say hello to each other."

She bowed in answer to his bow, smiled briefly, and said nothing.

The brawny servant with sideburns and a red waistcoat led him past the bear and up the staircase, its gleaming yellow wood covered by red carpets, then down an equally well-kept corridor to a large bedroom with a marble bath and windows looking out onto the park—a change from his room during previous visits, which had faced the courtyard. But the student didn't see a thing as he was led along. When he rode into the courtyard, a line from *Onegin* had been running through his head—*My uncle is a man of utmost principles*—but now another phrase eclipsed those words: *Christ, what a beautiful woman!*

He sang to himself while he shaved, washed, and changed, put on stirruped trousers—thinking all the while: What one would give for the love of a woman like that! How can there be such beautiful creatures pushing old people around in wheelchairs!

And soon his thoughts grew wild: I'll stay for a month, maybe two, and secretly befriend her. We'll grow intimate, I'll gain her love—and then, *Be my wife—I'm yours forever!* Mother, aunt, and uncle—they're all amazed when I announce our love and our plans to join our lives. They try to dissuade me, argue, shout, break down in tears. They curse and damn us, write me out of the will—and it's nothing. *I'll do anything for you.* . . .

But later, as he ran downstairs to his aunt and uncle—their rooms were on the first floor—the student thought: What nonsense gets into your head! You could come up with a reason to stay, you could start courting her secretly, even pretend you were madly in love, but would anything come of it? And if anything did come of it, what then? How would you get out of it? Would you marry—actually marry her?

He sat for an hour with his aunt and uncle in the latter's huge study, which contained a huge desk, a huge ottoman covered with fabrics from Turkestan, and little tables with inlaid ashtrays. The wall behind the ottoman was decorated with a rug and a pair of crossed swords from the east; above the fireplace, in a rosewood frame with a little golden crown, stood a large photograph of the tsar, which he'd signed with his own, free hand: Aleksandr.

"I'm so glad to see you again," said the student, thinking of the nurse. "It's so wonderful here, and I'll be so sorry to leave."

"Who's hurrying you? Stay as long as you like—where do you need to go?" His uncle answered.

"Of course, of course," his aunt said distractedly.

As he sat and chatted, the student waited impatiently: Now, now she'll come in—the maid will announce that tea is ready in the dining room, and she'll come to wheel uncle away. . . . But the servants rolled a table into the study with a silver teapot and a spirit lamp, and his aunt filled their cups herself. Then he clung to the hope that she would bring the general some odd dose of medicine. . . . But the nurse never appeared.

"To hell with her then," the student thought as he left the

study and wandered into the dining room, where a servant was closing the blinds on the tall, sun-filled windows. In the hallway to the right, the glassy tips of a piano's legs caught the evening light and made it lie like little candle flames on the hardwood floor. He glanced in that direction, then aimlessly headed to the left, through the living room into the den. From there he went onto the porch, descended to the yard, walked around the brilliant, variegated flower beds, and started down a shady path between two rows of trees. . . . It was still hot in the sun. He had two hours to wait until dinner.

At seven-thirty a gong rang out in the vestibule. The dining room was festively lit with a chandelier. He arrived alone to find a fat, clean-shaven cook in a starched white uniform; a butler with sunken cheeks, white gloves, and tails; and a little maid who looked as dainty and refined as a Frenchwoman standing near a table by the wall. A moment later his aunt came swaying into the room: grey and powdered as a queen, she wore a dress of pale yellow silk with creamy lace and a pair of tight silk shoes that displayed her bulging ankles. Finally the nurse appeared—but she glided from the room as soon as the general had been arranged at the table. He had time only to notice a peculiarity about her eyes: she never blinked. With quick, shallow little strokes, the general made the sign of the cross over his light grey, double-breasted uniform; the student and his aunt ardently crossed themselves while still standing, then solemnly took their seats and spread their brilliant napkins on their laps. The general's damp, sparse, carefully combed hair and his pale, well-scrubbed skin made the hopelessness of his condition more obvious than ever, but he ate a great deal and talked tirelessly about the current war against Japan, shrugging his shoulders and muttering, *Why the hell did we start it anyway?* They drank red and white wine from Prince Golitsyn—an old friend of the general's—and ate scalding eelpout soup, rare roast beef, new potatoes seasoned with dill. The cook unveiled each new dish with the self-importance of a deity; the butler served them with insulting indifference, and the maid took mincing little steps around the room as she assisted him. The student talked, answered questions, nodded with a smile—but the same ridiculous ideas he'd entertained while dressing for dinner continued to play inside his head, like nonsense ceaselessly repeated by a parrot: Where does she eat? With the servants? Again he waited for the moment she'd appear, roll uncle away, then meet him somewhere, let him say a few words. . . . But after wheeling the general from the dining room, she disappeared for good.

During the night he could hear the careful, precise songs of mockingbirds in the park; the flower beds were wet with dew, and he could smell their dampness in the fresh, cold air that drifted through the windows and cooled the sheets of good Dutch linen on his bed. Lying in the dark, the student decided it was time to sleep and rolled onto his side—but suddenly he lifted his head from the pillow. While undressing he had noticed a small door near his bed; curious, he'd opened it and discovered a second door, which was locked on the other side. Now someone was walking quietly, doing something secretive behind that door. Holding his breath, he slipped out of bed, opened the first door, and listened: something clinked softly on the floor. The student went cold. Could it be her room? Peering through the keyhole, he saw a light and the edge of a woman's dressing table—then his view was blocked by something white. It must be her room! Whose else could it be? The maid didn't live upstairs, and Marya Ilinishna, his aunt's old helper, slept near the main bedroom on the first floor. This discovery hit him like an illness:

she was just beyond the wall—just a few feet away, and still he couldn't reach her! The student slept badly and woke up late, his mind already feverish with images of her transparent nightshirt, her slippers, and her naked feet. "I should leave right now," he thought to himself, lighting up a cigarette.

They all had coffee in their separate rooms the next morning. He drank his while wearing a big nightshirt and a silk bathrobe that belonged to his uncle. He left the robe open and sat staring at his body, dismayed by its futility.

The dining room was gloomy and dull when he had breakfast with his aunt. The weather was bad. A strong wind shook the trees outside, and dark clouds clotted the sky.

"Well, darling, I'm leaving you," his aunt announced, getting up and crossing herself. "Try to entertain yourself as best you can, and forgive your uncle and me—we keep to ourselves until teatime. What a shame it's going to rain—you could have gone for a ride."

"Don't worry, aunt, I'll do some reading," he answered cheerfully, and headed for the den, where all the walls were lined with bookshelves.

Passing through the living room, he glanced out the window, wondering if he should order a horse to be saddled despite the weather. But a variety of rain clouds hung on the horizon, and the sky above the swaying trees had turned an unpleasant metallic blue among lilac-colored thunderheads. The den smelled of sweet cigar smoke; he glanced at a few superbly bound spines, then sat down, sinking helplessly into the plush leather of one of the couches that lined three walls of the room: *Truly hellish boredom.* If only he could see her, talk to her, find out what her voice was like, what kind of personality she had. Was she stupid? Or just the opposite—very in control, playing the role of a modest girl until just the right moment. Probably very guarded, and very aware of her worth. And probably stupid all the same. . . . But what a beauty! And again I'll have to sleep right next to her! He got up and opened the glass door, stepped outside toward the stone stairs that led to the garden. For a moment he could hear the trilling of the mockingbirds above the rustling leaves, but then a cold wind surged through a stand of young trees to his left, and he scrambled back inside. The room grew dark and the wind tore at the trees, bending their fresh, green branches. Sharp bursts of rain began to streak and flash across the windows and the glass door.

"They aren't bothered at all!" he said out loud, still listening to the trilling of the mockingbirds, whose songs seemed to gather in the wind and sail into the room. And immediately he heard a calm, impassive voice.

"Good day."

The nurse was standing before him. "I've come for a book," she said with friendly nonchalance as he gaped at her. "Reading's my only pleasure," she added with a smile, and walked toward the shelves.

"Hello—I didn't hear you come in," he mumbled.

"Very soft rugs." She turned around as she spoke and looked at him for a long time with her grey, unblinking eyes.

"And what do you like to read?" he asked, meeting her glance a little more boldly.

"Right now I'm reading Maupassant, Octave Mirbeau . . ."

"Of course—all women like Maupassant. He writes only about love."

"And what could be better than that?" Her voice was unassuming; a quiet smile played in her eyes.

"Love, love," he said, sighing. "There are surprising en-
counters, but . . . What is your full name, nurse?"

"Katerina Nikolayevna. And yours?"

"You can call me Pavlik," he answered, growing even more
bold.

"You want me to use pet names for you—just like your
aunt?"

"I'd be very happy to have an aunt like you. But for now I'm
just your unlucky neighbor."

"Is it really such bad luck?"

"I heard you last night. Your room, it turns out, is right next
to mine."

She laughed indifferently. "I heard you too. It's bad manners, you know, to peep through keyholes and listen at a woman's
door."

"But you're so excessively beautiful!" he said, staring stubbornly at her grey eyes, her light complexion, and the dark,
glossy hair under her white kerchief.

"Do you think so? And you'd forbid such excess?"

"I would. Your arms alone could make me lose my mind."

He caught her hand with playful daring as he spoke. Standing with her back to the shelves, she glanced over his shoulder
into the living room, then looked at him with a strange, slightly
mocking expression, as if to say: *Well—what now?* He tightened
his grip on her hand, pulled down on it, and grabbed her by the
waist. She glanced over his shoulder again, tossed back her head
as if protecting her face from his kisses—and pressed her arcing
waist against his body. Struggling to breathe, he brought his
mouth to her half-parted lips, then moved toward the couch.
The nurse frowned and shook her head. "No, no—if we lie

down, we won't be able to see, or hear," she whispered, and then, her eyes growing dim, she slowly spread her legs apart. . . . A minute later he dropped his head against her shoulder. She remained standing, her teeth still clenched, then quietly freed herself from him and walked into the next room, projecting her indifferent voice over the pelting rain. "Oh, it's pouring—and all the windows are open upstairs."

The next morning he woke up in her bed. The sheets were still warm and disheveled from the night; she lay on her back with one hand behind her head and all her naked arm exposed. He looked happily into her unblinking eyes. The sharp scent that rose from her armpit made him almost giddy with desire.

Someone knocked hurriedly at the door.

"Who is it?" she asked calmly, without pushing him away. "Marya Ilinishna?"

"Yes, Katerina Nikolayevna, it's me."

"What's wrong?"

"Let me in, please—I'm afraid someone will hear me and run off to frighten the general's wife."

When he had slipped into his room, she unhurriedly turned the key in the lock.

"There's something wrong with his excellency. I think he needs an injection," Marya Ilinishna whispered as she entered. "Thank goodness the general's wife is still asleep—you must come right away. . . ."

Marya Ilinishna's eyes turned beady as a snake's while she spoke, for she'd caught sight of a man's slippers near the bed— the student had run away barefoot. Katerina Nikolayevna also saw the slippers—as well as Marya Ilinishna's eyes.

Before breakfast she went to the general's wife and said she had to leave for home right away: she lied calmly, saying she'd just received a letter from her father, in which he wrote that her brother had been badly wounded near Manchuria. Her father, a widower, was all alone in his grief. . . .

"Ah, of course—I understand," the general's wife said, having already learned everything from Marya Ilinishna. "You must go right away, of course. Just send a message from the station for Dr. Krivtsov. Tell him to come and stay with us until we find another nurse."

Then she knocked on the student's door and slipped him a little note: "It's all over. I'm leaving. The old lady saw your slippers by my bed. Don't think ill of me."

At breakfast his aunt was a little sad, but she spoke as if nothing were wrong. "Did you hear, the nurse is leaving for her father's house—he's all alone, and her brother's been terribly wounded. . . ."

"I heard, aunt. This wretched war's made everyone miserable. . . . What was wrong with uncle, anyway?"

"Oh, it was nothing, thank God. He's such a hypochondriac! He thought he was having a heart attack—but it was only indigestion."

At three o'clock they drove Antigone to the station in a troika. Pretending he was going out for a ride, the student ran onto the porch, as if by accident, just as she was leaving. He said goodbye without raising his eyes, ready to shout in despair. She waved her glove to him as she rode away in the carriage—her white kerchief was already gone, replaced by an elegant hat.

[1940]

Zoyka and Valeriya

IN THE WINTER Levitsky spent all of his free time at the Danilevskys' Moscow apartment, and in the summer he began to visit their dacha in the pine forest along the Kazan railway line.

He was in his fifth year at the university and was twenty-four years old, but at the Danilevskys' only the doctor referred to him as "colleague"; everyone else called him "Zhorzh" or "Zhorzhik." Lonely and prone to falling in love, he often attached himself to some familiar household and soon became a member of the family, visiting for days on end, sometimes from morning until night if his lessons allowed—and so it was with the Danilevskys. Not only the hostess but even the children—the plump Zoyka and the big-eared Grishka—treated him like some kind of distant, homeless relative. Outwardly he was simple and kind, quiet but obliging, always ready to respond if a word was directed toward him.

When patients came to see Danilevsky, an old woman in a nurse's uniform opened the door and ushered them into a big parlor furnished with rugs and imposing antique furniture; there she put on her glasses, picked up a pencil, and looked sternly at her appointment book. Some of the patients were then told the hour and the day of their future appointments; others were led through the tall doors of the reception room. Here they waited a long time to be called into yet another room, where a young assistant in a smock as white as sugar questioned and examined them. It was only after all of this that the patients finally reached Danilevsky himself in his big office where, along the back wall, there was a high bed on which some of the patients were made to lie in the most pitiful, awkward, and frightening positions: all of it confused and embarrassed the patients—the assistant and the woman in the hall, the shiny copper disk at the end of the pendulum that swung so gravely in the grandfather clock, the general air of importance that permeated the spacious, rich apartment, and the expectant silence of the waiting room, where no one dared to take an extra breath. All of the patients therefore believed that this was an eternally lifeless place, and they were sure that Danilevsky, who was tall, thick-set, and rather rude, must smile no more than once a year. But they were wrong: to the right of the entrance, a set of double doors led to the living quarters, and here there was almost constant noise from the guests. The samovar was never taken from the table, and the maid never stopped running, bringing more glasses and cups, a jar of jam, biscuits and white bread. Even during his receiving hours, Danilevsky would often sneak down the hall to drink tea with his visitors and talk about the patients, saying, "Ah, they can wait a bit—may the devil have their mothers," while the patients themselves sat quietly, convinced the doctor was busy with some critical case.

Once, while sitting this way, Danilevsky looked with a smile at Levitsky's stooped and skinny frame, his sunken stomach and his slightly crooked legs. "Tell the truth, colleague," he said, studying the young man's taut, freckled skin, his hawkish eyes and wiry red hair, "surely you have some eastern blood—Jewish maybe, or Caucasian?"

"None at all, Nikolay Grigoryevich, no Jewish blood," Levitsky answered with his unflagging eagerness to speak when spoken to. "There are some Ukrainian Levitskys, so, like you, I might have a little Ukrainian blood. And some Polish. And I hear from my grandfather there might be some Turkish. . . . But really, Allah only knows."

Danilevsky roared with laughter. "Ah, you see, I was right! Be careful ladies and girls—he's a Turk! Not at all the humble fellow you might take him for! And as we know, he loves like a Turk. Whose turn is it now, colleague? Who is the woman of your generous heart these days?"

"Dariya Tadiyevna," Levitsky answered with a simple-hearted smile, turning red as if a small flame were passing over his body. He often smiled and blushed this way.

Dariya Tadiyevna was a good-looking woman with a bluish down on her upper lip and along her cheeks. Still recovering from typhus, she wore a little cap of black silk as she half sat and half lay in an armchair nearby. Overhearing Levitsky, she was so charmingly embarrassed that her black-currant eyes seemed to disappear completely for a moment.

"Well?" she said. "That's not a secret to anyone. It's completely natural, since I have Eastern blood as well."

Then Grishka began to shout lustily, "They've been caught, they've been caught!" while Zoyka, screwing up her eyes, bolted into the next room and fell across the armrest of the couch.

That winter Levitsky really was secretly in love with Dariya Tadiyevna, and before her, he had felt something for Zoyka. She was only fourteen, but she was physically mature, especially when seen from behind, although the slightly blue knees below her short, plaid skirt were still as round and tender as a child's. A year ago they'd taken Zoyka out of school after Danilevsky diagnosed her with the early signs of some sort of brain disease, and since no one taught her anything at home, Zoyka lived in a state of carefree idleness without ever being bored. She felt such tenderness for people that she licked her lips whenever they came close. Her forehead was high and domed, her mouth was always damp, and her oily blue eyes expressed a naïve joy, as if the world were a constant, delightful surprise. For all her corpulence, Zoyka moved with a seductive grace, and the red ribbon tied in her shimmering, nut-brown hair made her only more appealing. She often sat in Levitsky's lap, and although she acted like an innocent child at such moments, she probably understood quite well what he was suffering in secret as he held her plump body and tried to keep from looking at those bare knees below her checkered skirt. Sometimes he couldn't control himself and kissed her on the cheek as if joking, and she closed her eyes and smiled in a languid, teasing way. Once she secretly told Levitsky what she alone in the world knew about her mother—she was in love with the young doctor Titov! Mama's forty, but she looks very young, and she's so thin—just like a girl with noble blood, and both of them—she and the doctor—they're so beautiful and tall! Then Levitsky became inattentive to her, for Dariya Tadiyevna had begun to appear in the house. Zoyka pretended to be even happier, even more carefree, and sometimes she would throw herself on Dariya Tadiyevna with a shout, kissing her and hating her so intensely that when the woman later fell ill, Zoyka daily awaited the joyous news of her death. Then she waited for her to leave—and for summer, knowing Levitsky would be freed from his studies to visit the dacha her family had kept for three years in the forest near the Kazan railway line: in secret she was hunting him.

Then summer came, and he began to visit for two or three days at a time each week. But soon another guest arrived—papa's niece from Kharkov, Valeriya Ostrogradskaya, whom neither Grishka nor Zoyka had ever seen. Levitsky was sent to Moscow early one morning to meet her at Kursk station, and he returned from the dacha train stop not on his bicycle but with her in a cart, looking tired, hollow-eyed, and joyously excited. It was obvious he'd fallen in love with her before the train even left Moscow, and she treated him like her subject as he carried her bags to the house. As soon as she ran onto the porch to meet mother, however, she forgot all about Levitsky and didn't notice him again for the rest of the day. To Zoyka she was completely incomprehensible—while sorting her things in her room, and later, while having breakfast on the balcony, she would talk a great deal, then suddenly fall silent, as if lost in her own thoughts. But she was a true Ukrainian beauty! And Zoyka stuck to her with unshakable determination.

"Did you bring leather boots? And a brocade kerchief? Will you put them on? May I call you Valechka?"

Even without her Ukrainian apparel, she was very attractive

indeed: shapely and strong, with thick dark hair and velvety eyebrows that almost joined in the middle. Her unnerving eyes were the color of black blood and her face had a dark, warm glow from the sun. She had shiny white teeth and lips like ripe cherries. Her hands were small but strong and evenly tanned, like meat that had been delicately smoked. And what shoulders! And how easy it was to see the pink, silk straps of the camisole that touched those shoulders under her thin white blouse! Her skirt was short and simple, but it fit her to perfection! Zoyka was too carried away to be jealous of Levitsky, who had stopped going to Moscow altogether, and now never left Valeriya's side, happy because she'd grown more friendly, called him by his first name, and constantly ordered him to do something. Then the full, hot days of summer began, and more and more guests came from Moscow. Zoyka noticed that Levitsky had been dismissed: he often sat with mother now, helping her clean raspberries, while Valeriya had fallen in love with Dr. Titov, the same man whom mother secretly loved. Something strange had happened to Valeriya in general—when the guests were gone, she no longer changed from one elegant blouse into another, and sometimes she walked around from morning until night wearing mother's peignoir and looking mildly disgusted. Zoyka was terribly curious—did she kiss Levitsky before falling in love with Titov? Grishka swore that he had seen her walking once in the alley of spruces with Levitsky after swimming. She wore a towel on her head like a turban, and Levitsky stumbled along behind her, carrying a wet bath sheet and saying something over and over until she stopped, and he suddenly grabbed her by the shoulders and kissed her lips.

"I hid behind the trees so they couldn't see me," Grishka said excitedly, his eyes bulging out. "I saw everything. She looked very pretty—only red all over—it was still hot and she swam too much—you know how she always stays in the water for at least two hours a day—I spied on her then too—she looked like a Naiad when she was nude in the water! And he kept talking and talking—he really is like a Turk."

Grishka swore it was true, but he loved to make up stupid stories, and Zoyka believed and didn't believe.

On Saturdays and Sundays even the morning trains from Moscow were crowded with people coming to visit dachas. Sometimes a pleasant rain fell through the sunlight, and the green railroad cars were washed clean and shone as if new, and the white puffs of smoke from the engine became especially soft, and the rounded tops of the graceful pines that stood along the tracks seemed to extend even farther into the bright air above the passing trains. The arriving passengers competed for carts on hot, packed sand near the station, then rode happily down lanes that had been cut into the woods, the sky like streamers over their heads. Soon a mood of pure country bliss took over the forest that spread in all directions and sheltered the dry, undulating earth. When the hosts took their Moscow guests for walks, they'd boast that bears were the only thing missing in the forest; they'd recite, *"The dark woods smell of pitch and wild berries"* and shout out "hello" to one another, enjoying their idle summer days and their free-spirited clothes—their long peasant shirts with embroidered hems and colorful braided belts, their canvas caps. Indeed, it was not easy to recognize a Moscow acquaintance—a professor or the bearded, bespectacled editor of some journal—as he wandered in such clothes.

In this festive mood of summer living, Levitsky was doubly miserable, feeling pitiful, deceived, and extraneous from dawn until dusk. He wondered the same thing constantly: Why, why did she take him in so quickly and so ruthlessly, why did she make him a friend, and then a slave, and then a lover to be satisfied with the always rare and unexpected joy of mere kisses? Why did she call him "thou" one day and "you" the next? And how could she have the cruelty to so simply, so casually forget him after the first day of her acquaintance with Titov? He burned with shame over his ridiculous lingering at the house and planned to disappear in a day's time—run to Moscow, hide his disgraced and idiotic dacha love, which had grown obvious even to the servants.

But as soon as he began to think this way, he wound up paralyzed by the mere memory of her mouth. If she happened to pass by while he was sitting alone on the balcony, she would casually say something meaningless—"Where is my aunt? Have you seen her?"—and he would hurry to answer in the same tone while ready to scream from the pain. One day she saw Zoyka sitting in his lap—what did it matter to her? But she narrowed her eyes in rage and shouted, "You disgusting girl! Don't you dare climb into men's laps!"—and he was ecstatic. Jealousy! That was jealousy! Meanwhile, Zoyka sensed every moment it was possible to throw her arms around his neck in some empty room, stare at him with her shining eyes, lick her lips and whisper, "Dear, dear, dear." Once she caught his lips so neatly with her wet mouth that he couldn't think of Zoyka for the rest of the day without shudders of desire, and horror. "What's wrong with me! How can I face Nikolay Grigoryevich and Klavdiya Aleksandrovna!"

The dacha grounds were large, like those of a country estate. To the right of the courtyard entrance stood an empty stable with a hayloft, next to it the servants' wing extended to the kitchen. Birch trees and lindens glimmered in the background. To the left, old pines grew luxuriantly in firm, uneven soil; swing sets and giants' steps stood in a patch of grass below them. A smooth lawn for croquet lay farther on, already at the wood's edge. The house was large as well; it stood right at the end of the driveway with a disorienting mixture of garden and forest spreading out behind it. An elegant avenue of old spruces ran through this confusion from the back porch to the bathing house on the pond. With or without their guests, the hosts always sat on the front balcony, which was set back into the house and shaded from the sun. One hot Sunday morning only Levitsky was there with mother. Many guests had come, and, as always when guests were present, the day seemed especially festive. Their new dresses shining in the sun, maids trotted back and forth across the courtyard between the house and the kitchen, where hurried preparations were under way for breakfast. Five people had come to visit: a dark-faced, bilious writer who was both excessively serious and passionately devoted to games; a fifty-year-old professor with little legs and a face like Socrates'; his newly wedded wife and former student, who was thin, blond, and twenty years old; a small, chic woman whom everyone called "the wasp" because of her lean figure, her touchiness, and her vicious temper; and Titov, whom Danilevsky referred to as "the insolent gentleman." All of the guests, as well as Valeriya and Danilevsky himself, were under the pines near the forest. Danilevsky sat smoking a cigar in an armchair in the limpid shade. The children, the professor's wife, and the writer were riding the giants' steps while the professor, the wasp, Titov, and Valeriya ran around the croquet lawn, hitting balls with their mallets, shouting back and forth, arguing about the game. Levitsky and mother were listening to them. Earlier, Levitsky had tried to join the group, but as soon as he'd approached, Valeriya had driven him off—"My aunt is pitting the cherries all alone; why don't you go and help her?" He'd stood for a moment, smiling awkwardly and looking at her, the way she held a mallet in her hand and bent over a wooden ball, the way her tussore skirt hung over her taut calves in stockings of pale yellow silk, the way her breasts pulled heavily at her light blouse while its fabric revealed her round shoulders—dark from the sun and tinged slightly pink by the rose-colored straps of her camisole.

He'd looked, and then he'd plodded back to the balcony. He was especially pitiful that morning, and mother—who was always calm and even-tempered, with her young, serene face, her clear gaze, and her own secret pain from the voices under the trees—watched him from the corner of her eye.

"We'll never get our hands clean now," she said, sticking a little gilded fork into a cherry with her bloodied fingers. "And you, Zhorzhik, always manage to spill all over yourself. Dearest, why are you still wearing a jacket? It's so hot you could easily wear just a belted shirt. And you haven't shaved in ten days. . . ."

He knew that a reddish stubble had grown over his hollow cheeks, that his only white coat was grimy from continuous wear, that his student's pants had developed an unsightly sheen, and that his shoes were cloudy with dust. He knew that he slouched as he sat there with his sunken stomach and his scrawny chest.

"You're right, Klavdiya Aleksandrovna," he said, blushing. "You are absolutely right. I've let myself go terribly—I look like an escaped convict. I've exploited your kindness despicably. Forgive me, please, if you can. I'll pull myself together today. I should have left for Moscow long ago: I've already overstayed my welcome here, plaguing everyone. I've decided to leave tomorrow. A friend has invited me to Mogilev—he says it's a beautiful place."

Hearing Titov shouting at Valeriya, he bent lower over the

table. "No, no, my lady, that's against the rules! It's your fault if you don't know how to hold one ball with your foot and hit with your mallet. You don't get to try twice. . . ."

At breakfast he felt as if everyone at the table had somehow crawled inside his body. They were eating, talking, making witty jokes, and bursting out with laughter inside him. Afterward they all went to rest in the avenue of spruces, where the maids had put pillows and rugs in the shade among beds of slippery pine needles. He walked through the courtyard's hot sunlight to the stable, climbed the wall ladder to the loft, and flopped down into the old hay and the semi-dark. Trying to decide something, he lay on his stomach and stared intently at a fly that had landed on a piece of straw near his face. At first the fly moved its front legs together in a quick, crisscross motion as if washing. But then it started struggling in some unnatural way to pull its hind legs forward. Suddenly someone ran inside and slammed the door: turning, he saw Zoyka in the light of the dormer window. She jumped toward him and sank into the hay on her stomach. Panting, she stared at him with somehow frightened eyes. "Zhorzhik dear, I have to tell you something," she whispered, "something exciting for you—something wonderful."

"What is it, Zoyechka?" he said, sitting up.

"You'll see, but first you have to kiss me. Right away," and she kicked her legs in the hay, exposing her full thighs.

He was too worn out by misery to suppress an unhealthy feeling of tenderness. "Zoyechka," he said, "you alone love me, and I love you too. But you shouldn't do this, please. . . ."

She kicked even harder. "You have to—right now!"

She put her head on his chest. He saw her shiny, fresh brown hair under the red ribbon, smelled its fragrance, and nestled his face in it. Suddenly she screamed, "Ah!" and grabbed the back of her skirt.

He jumped to his feet. "What is it?"

"Something bit me!" She dropped her head in the hay and began to wail. "What was it! Look, quickly!"

She flung her skirt up her back and tugged down her underwear. "What is it? Am I bleeding?"

"No, I don't see anything, Zoyechka."

"What do you mean!" She sobbed. "Blow on it! It hurts!"

He blew, and then he kissed the soft, cool flesh of her buttocks. He kissed her greedily until she jumped up, teary-eyed and almost insane from the pleasure.

"I fooled you!" she shouted. "I fooled you! And for that, I'll tell you my secret: Titov dumped her. Grishka and I heard everything. They were walking on the balcony while we were sitting on the floor in the living room, behind the armchairs. And he was very insulting. He says to her, 'My lady, I'm not one of those you can lead around by the nose. I don't even love you. I'll start to if you earn my affection, but for now, there won't be any declarations.' Isn't that great? It's just what she deserves!"

Then she rushed to the ladder and scurried down. He stared after her. "I'm sick! Hanging is too good for me!" he said loudly, still feeling her flesh on his lips.

Evening was quiet at the estate. The guests had left at six, and now the warm dusk, the cooking smoke from the kitchen, and the soothing scent of lindens blooming in the yard brought a mood of peace and quiet domesticity to the house. But even in that peaceful happiness—in the dusk, among the smells—it remained: the ever-promising torture of her presence, her existence near him . . . the soul-wrenching pain of his love and her merciless indifference, her absence. . . . Where is she? He came down from the balcony and, hearing the steady squeak of a swing, walked toward the pines. Yes, it's her. He stopped, watching the way she sailed up and down, always stretching the cords to their limit, always trying to reach the last height, and pretending not to notice him. The rings squeal and she flies up, disappears among the branches, and shoots back down, her hem fluttering as she pumps with her legs. Oh, if only he could catch her! Grab her, strangle, rape her!

"Valeriya Andreyevna, be careful!"

She only swings harder, as if she hasn't heard.

During dinner on the balcony they laughed and argued about the guests while sitting under hot, bright lamps. Her laughter was bitter and unnatural; she ate *tvorog* with sour cream greedily, again never glancing in his direction. Only Zoyka was silent, her eyes shining as she looked at him with the knowledge that they alone shared.

Everyone went to bed early. Not a single light was left burning, and everything around turned dark and lifeless. He slipped into his room after supper and began stuffing his clothes into a shoulder bag, thinking, "I'll take the bicycle out quietly, ride straight to the station. I'll sleep somewhere in the woods until the first morning train. . . . But no, I can't do that. . . . God knows what they'd make of it. They'd say he ran off like a little boy, didn't say goodbye to anyone. I'll have to wait until tomorrow and leave casually, as if nothing had happened. 'Goodbye my dear Nikolay Grigoryevich, goodbye dear Klavdiya Aleksandrovna! Thank you, thanks for everything. Yes, yes, they say Mogilev is a beautiful city. . . . Zoyechka, take care. Grow and be happy! Grisha, let me shake your hand like a gentleman. Valeriya Andreyevna, all the best. Try to remember me kindly' . . .

No, 'try to remember me kindly' is stupid, tactless—like some kind of hint about something. . . ."

Certain that he couldn't fall asleep if he tried, Levitsky came down from the balcony to walk on the station road, hoping to wear himself out. But in the courtyard he stopped: warm dusk, sweet silence, a whiteness in the sky from small, innumerable stars. . . . He started again and stopped again, lifting his head: the stars go farther and farther into the sky, and then there's terror, blue-black dark, a bottomless gorge. . . . Then there's silence, peace, a vast wilderness that no one understands, and all the lifeless, pointless beauty of the world—all the mute, eternal psalms of night. . . . And he, alone, face to face with it—somewhere in the chasm between sky and earth. He began to pray without words for some small act of pity, some sign of heavenly compassion, and with bitter joy he felt himself freed from his body, felt himself linked to the sky. Then he looked back at the house. Trying to stay as he was, he looked at the starlight hanging in the black glass of the windows—hanging in her window. . . . Is she asleep, or lying in a daze, thinking about Titov? Yes, it's her turn now. . . .

The house loomed large and indistinct among the shadows. He walked around it to a small field between the rear balcony and two rows of ink-black, motionless spruces: they seemed menacing now, with their sharp tips so close to the stars. In the darkness below them hung the greenish, yellow flares of fireflies. Something white was lying on the balcony: he stopped and peered into the darkness, then started with surprise as a voice free of all emotion said, "Why are you wandering around in the night?" Dumbfounded, he moved forward and saw that she was sitting in a rocking chair, wearing the old silver shawl that all of Danilevsky's female guests put on when they stayed the night.

"Why aren't you asleep?" he stammered in confusion.

She sat without answering for a moment, then rose and came soundlessly down from the balcony, sliding the shawl up her shoulders as she moved.

"Take a walk with me."

He walked behind and then beside her in the hushed, still darkness of that avenue between the trees, where now, more than ever, it seemed something had been hidden. And how could it be? How was he walking alone with her again in this avenue at this hour? And that shawl again, always slipping from her shoulders, always pricking his fingers slightly with its silk fibers as he pulls it around her.

"Why do you torture me this way?" he said, struggling to overcome a spasm in his throat.

She shook her head. "I don't know. Be quiet."

He grew slightly bolder and raised his voice. "Yes, why—what for? Why did you . . ."

She caught his hand and pressed it. "Be quiet."

"Valya, I don't understand anything. . . ."

She let go of his hand and glanced at one of the spruces at the end of the avenue. The outline of its limbs formed a wide black triangle.

"Do you remember this place? I kissed you for the first time here. Now I want you to kiss me here for the last time. . . ."

Then she ducked under the branches and flung her shawl on the ground. "Come here."

As soon as it was over, she pushed him away with sharp revulsion, lowered her knees, and lay with her legs still spread, her hands stretched along her hips. He sprawled beside her, his face against the ground, pine needles turning damp with his warm tears. The forest had grown completely silent and still, and, like a slice of red melon suspended in the dead of night, the late moon hung motionless above the darkened fields.

When he returned to his room, he glanced at the clock with bloodshot, swollen eyes and panicked at the time: twenty minutes to two! He carried the bicycle down from the balcony as quickly and quietly as he could, then wheeled it hurriedly across the yard. Past the gate, he jumped on and leaned low over the handlebars, pedaling wildly and bouncing over potholes in the sandy soil. The pines that lined the lane seemed to run toward him as he rode, their black trunks flickering against the predawn sky. "I'll miss it!" He wiped the sweat from his forehead with the crook of his arm and began to pedal even harder: an express from Moscow rolls past the station without stopping at 2:15—only a few minutes left! At the end of the lane, he suddenly caught sight of the station's silhouette in the early morning light, which still resembled dusk. There it is! He turned left onto a road that ran parallel to the tracks, then veered right to the crossing. There he ducked under the signal arm without stopping, swerved hard onto the tracks, started to roll down the incline: rattling over the crossties between the rails, he headed straight for the blinding lamp of the oncoming engine as it roared up the hill.

[1940]

In Paris

HIS SHORT, auburn hair was shot with grey, but if he wore a hat while walking down the street or riding on the subway, his fresh, clean-shaven face and his tall, thin frame—held straight and upright in a long raincoat—made him seem no more than forty. Still, his light eyes contained a kind of dry sadness, and he spoke and carried himself like a man who'd lived through much. Once he'd rented a farm in Provence, and now, while living in Paris, he liked to repeat the caustic aphorisms he'd heard so often in the countryside, smiling wryly as he inserted them into his always concise speech. Many people knew that his wife had left him when they were still in Constantinople, and that his soul had not healed since then. He never revealed that secret wound to anyone, but sometimes he couldn't help hinting at it, and if the conversation turned to women, he would joke unpleasantly:

"Rien n'est plus difficile que de reconnaître un bon melon et une femme de bien."

One damp evening in late fall he stopped for supper at a small Russian restaurant in one of the dark alleys on Passy. At the front of the restaurant was a kind of delicatessen, and he paused instinctively before its window, where pink, cone-shaped bottles of Rowanberry vodka and rectangular yellow flasks of *zubrovka* had been arranged on the sill beside a dish of dried-out little pies, a dish of greying mincemeat cutlets, a box of halvah, and a can of sprats; farther on he could see a counter set with appetizers, behind which frowned the unappealing face of the Russian owner. It was light inside the shop, and something drew him from the dark alley and its cold, oily-looking stones toward that light. He entered, bowed to the hostess, and walked into the empty, dimly lit dining room, where tables were covered with white paper. There he slowly hung his hat and his long coat on the rack, sat down at a table in the farthest corner, and began to read an endless list of appetizers and main courses while distractedly rubbing his hands together. Part of the menu was typed, and part was written in a violet-colored ink that had begun to smudge on the greasy paper. Suddenly the lights were turned on in his corner, and he saw a woman approaching the table with detached complaisance. Wearing a white, lacy apron over a black dress, she looked about thirty; her eyes and hair were also black.

"Bonsoir, monsieur," she said in a pleasant voice.

As he looked at her, he realized she was beautiful, and her beauty flustered him. "Bonsoir. . . . But you're Russian, aren't you?" he answered awkwardly.

"Oh, yes. I'm sorry—speaking French to the customers has become a habit."

"Do you really get a lot of French customers here?"

"Quite a lot. And they always ask about *zubrovka*, blinis—even borscht. Have you decided?"

"No. . . . There's so much here. . . . What do you recommend?"

She began to recite. "Today we have sailor's shchi and Cossack rissole. . . . If you'd like, you could also have veal chops or Karski shashlik."

"Excellent. I'll have the shchi and rissole."

She lifted up a little notebook that hung from her belt and began to write with a pencil stub. Her hands looked very white and delicate, and although the dress was old, it obviously came from a good shop.

"Would you care for vodka?"

"Please—it's awfully damp out there."

"And what appetizers would you like? The Danube herring is excellent. And the red caviar is fresh. We have *korkunovsky* half-sour pickles as well."

He looked at her again—a very pretty white apron with lace over a black dress, the graceful outline of a young, strong woman's breasts beneath it. . . . She wore no lipstick, but her mouth looked full and fresh. Her hair was parted in the middle and wrapped around her head in just a simple braid, but the flesh of her white hands was sleek, and her glistening, slightly pink nails revealed a recent manicure.

"What appetizers would I like?" he said with a smile, slightly flustered by her courteous attention. "I'll just have the herring and hot potatoes, if that's all right."

"And what wine shall I bring?"

"Red. The house wine."

She wrote in her notebook and brought a carafe of water from the neighboring table. "No, merci," he said, shaking his head. "I don't drink water, especially with wine. *L'eau gâte le vin comme la charrette le chemin et la femme—l'âme.*"

"What a nice opinion you have of us!" she said indifferently as she left for his vodka and herring. He watched her walk gracefully away, watched her black dress swaying as she moved. . . . Yes, her good manners and her indifference, all her modest gestures are suited to a waitress. . . . But how does she afford those expensive shoes? Probably some well-to-do elderly *"ami."* . . . Because of her he was more animated that night than he had been in years—and this realization annoyed him. Yes, from day to day, from year to year, you wait in secret for only one thing—that moment when you'll stumble onto happy love. Ultimately it is this hope alone that enables you to live, and all of it's in vain.

He returned the next day and sat down at the same table. She was busy at first, taking an order from two Frenchmen, repeating as she wrote in her notebook: "Caviar rouge, salad russe. . . . Deaux shashliks. . . ."

She went into the kitchen, then returned and approached him with a slight smile, as if he were an old acquaintance.

"Good evening. I'm glad you liked it here."

Smiling, he rose to his feet. "Hello, yes, I liked it very much. . . . Can I ask your name?"

"Olga Aleksandrovna. And yours, if I may ask?"

"Nikolay Platonych."

They shook hands, and she raised her little notebook.

"Today we have a wonderful rassolnik. Our cook's remarkable—you know, he served on Prince Aleksandr Mikhaylovich's yacht. . . ."

"Well then, the rassolnik must be good—I'll have that. . . . Have you worked here long?"

"About two months."

[163]

"And where did you work before?"

"Before this I was a sales clerk at Printemps."

"They must have laid you off—when they cut back on staff?"

"Yes, I would have stayed there if I'd had the chance."

Then the money doesn't come from an "*ami*," he thought happily. "Are you married?"

"Yes."

"What does your husband do?"

"He works in Yugoslavia now. He fought for the White Army—like you, I imagine."

"Yes, I fought in the civil war—and in the Great War before it as well."

"I could tell right away. You're probably a general," she said, smiling.

"I was. Now I'm writing a history of the wars for some foreign publishers. . . . But how did you wind up alone?"

"I just wound up that way—alone."

On his third night in the restaurant, he asked: "Do you like the cinema?"

"Sometimes it's interesting," she said, setting a bowl of borscht in front of him.

"They say there's an excellent film showing at the Étoile. Would you like to see it? You don't work every day, do you?"

"Merci. I'm free on Mondays."

"Well, let's go on Monday. What's today? Saturday? Day after tomorrow then. Does that sound possible?"

"Yes, that sounds good. But tomorrow—you won't be coming in?"

"No, I'm going out of town to see some people. Why do you ask?"

"I don't know. . . . It's strange—I guess I've gotten used to you somehow."

He looked at her with gratitude and blushed. "I've grown used to you as well. . . . It's so rare in this world—that you meet someone. . . ."

Hurriedly he changed the topic. "Well then, day after tomorrow. Where should we meet? Where do you live?"

"Near the Motte-Picquet stop."

"Well, that's perfect—the Étoile is on the same line. I'll be waiting for you at the subway exit at 8:30 sharp."

"Merci."

He bowed lightheartedly. "*C'est moi qui vous remercie.* Put the kids to bed and have an evening out," he added, to see if she had children.

"I haven't experienced the joy of children yet, thank God," she said, and smoothly whisked away his dirty plates.

Touched by her words, he walked home frowning. *I guess I've gotten used to you somehow.* Yes, maybe this is it—that long-awaited meeting, that happiness. But it is late, late. *Le bon Dieu envoie toujours des culottes à ceux qui n'ont pas de derrière.* . . .

It was raining Monday evening, and the Paris sky was filled with a turbid, reddish haze. He stopped at a café on Chaussée de la Muette and ate just a sandwich with a glass of beer, hoping she would dine with him later on Montparnasse. Then he hailed a cab, lit a cigarette, and rode toward the subway stop Étoile.

Near the station exit he got out and started down the side-walk in the rain; his taxi driver—a chubby fellow with purple cheeks—waited trustingly with the car. A hot, damp breeze was streaming from the station doors; throngs of people in dark coats climbed the stairs, opening umbrellas as they walked. Behind him, a street vendor called out the names of the evening newspapers in a low, raspy voice that sounded like a duck quacking in the drizzle. Suddenly she appeared in the crowd; he felt elated as he rushed to meet her.

"Olga Aleksandrovna . . ."

She looked elegant and stylish in her long, black evening dress; and her dark, painted eyes expressed a kind of easy self-assurance that he hadn't seen before in the restaurant. She held the gown's hem as she approached, and then gracefully extended her free hand, a small umbrella dangling from her arm. He folded back her glove and kissed the back of her pale wrist. "She's in evening wear," he thought, feeling even happier. "She's planning on us dining out."

"Poor thing, have you been waiting long?"

"No, I just arrived. I have a taxi waiting. . . ."

And he climbed into that half-dark, damp-smelling cab with a feeling of excitement that had left his life long ago. The driver took a sharp turn hard, and light from a street lamp suddenly flooded the interior as the cab swayed; instinctively he held her steady by the waist, smelling the powder on her cheek, glimpsing the outline of her full knees beneath the evening dress, her shining eyes and damp, red lips: the woman next to him was nothing like the one who waited tables.

They spoke quietly in the darkened theatre while looking at a brilliant white screen where airplanes flew at angles through the sky and descended with a noisy drone toward the clouds.

"Do you live alone, or with a girlfriend?" he asked.

"Alone. It's awful, really. The hotel's quite clean and warm, but—you know, it's one of those places men bring girls for a night, or for an hour. I live on the sixth floor, and there's no elevator, of course. The carpet in the stairwell stops two stories down from me. . . . On rainy nights it's terribly depressing. You open a window and there's not a soul to see, the entire town seems dead. Somewhere below you, God knows where, there's one streetlight in the rain. . . . But you're a bachelor—you must live in a hotel too."

"I have a little apartment on Passy—I live alone there, a long-term Parisian. I lived in Provence once, years ago—rented a farm there. I wanted to get away from everything—and everyone. And I wanted to live by my own labor. But the labor was unbearable. I hired a Cossack to help me, and he turned out to be a drunk—a gloomy, frightening drunk. I tried to raise poultry and rabbits, but they all died off, and my mule—a very cunning, very nasty animal—practically ate me alive. . . . But mostly it was the utter loneliness. . . . My wife left me when we were still in Constantinople."

"You're joking?"

"Not at all. It's a very ordinary story. *Qui se marie par amour a bonnes nuits et mauvais jours.* And I didn't have many days or nights—we'd only been married for a year before she left."

"Where is she now?"

"I don't know. . . ."

She didn't speak for a long time. On the screen some kind of Charlie Chaplin imitator was running with his feet splayed like an idiot; he wore ridiculous, battered shoes and a bowler hat cocked to the side.

"Yes, it must be awfully lonely," she said.

"It is. But what can you do? Just endure. *Patience— médecine des pauvres.*"

"A very sad medicine."

"So sad, in fact," he said with a slight smile, "that I'd even started looking at *Russia Illustrated*—it has a kind of dating section, you know—announcements from people looking for companions: 'A Russian girl from Latvia is bored and wishes to correspond with a sensitive Russian gentleman in Paris—photograph requested.' Or: 'A serious lady seeks serious correspondence with a sober gentleman over forty who likes the comforts of family life. He should be financially secure, gainfully employed as a chauffeur or some similar, reliable profession. She's an old-fashioned but attractive brunette, a widow with a nine-year-old son. Will answer all inquiries. . . .' All inquiries. . . . I know exactly how she feels."

"But don't you have friends, people you know?"

"No friends—and acquaintances are poor comfort."

"Who keeps house for you?"

"My household's very modest. I make my own coffee and lunch. In the evenings a *femme de ménage* comes."

She squeezed his hand. "Poor thing."

They sat this way a long time, drawn together by the gloom and the cramped seats, holding hands and pretending to look at the screen while a beam of light from the projectionist's booth hung like a chalky, bluish stripe above their heads. The Chaplin imitator was driving a broken-down car with a little chimney that smoked like a samovar; his battered hat rose and hovered above his head—a sign of shock and horror—as the jalopy sailed toward a telegraph pole and music blared over the loudspeaker. They were sitting in the balcony, and the floor below them— dark and hazy with the smoke of countless cigarettes—was like a pit resounding with raucous laughter and applause. He leaned toward her. "This film is quite tedious, isn't it? And there's so much smoke in here it's hard to breathe. Maybe we should go to dine somewhere on Montparnasse?" She nodded and began putting on her gloves.

Once more they rode in the half-dark cab. He watched the rain shimmer on the windows—and having seen it flash like uncut diamonds as it caught the streetlights' glare, having seen it fill with the neon that streamed like blood and mercury from electric billboards perched in the blackness overhead, he folded back her glove again and slowly kissed her hand. The same strange light seemed to glitter from behind her thick, coal-black lashes as she looked at him—and then, with love and sadness, leaned closer, brought her rich, sweet-tasting mouth to his.

At the Café Coupole they started with oysters and Anjou, then partridge and a red claret. Over coffee and yellow char-treuse they began to feel light-headed, and both smoked heavily; filters stained blood-red with lipstick quickly filled the ashtray. While she talked, he studied her slightly flushed face, feeling more and more enamored of her beauty.

"Tell the truth," she said, lightly pinching a tobacco crumb from the tip of her tongue. "You must have had a few rendezvous in Paris."

"I did—but you know the kind. Hotels at night, nothing more. And you?"

She paused. "There was one very unhappy episode. . . . But I don't want to talk about that. Just a little boy—a pimp, in essence. . . . But how did you and your wife split up?"

"Shamefully. She met a boy of her own, a handsome Greek who was extraordinarily rich. Two months later not a trace re-mained of that touching, innocent girl who'd idolized the White Army and everyone who served it. She began to dine with him in the most expensive pigsty in Pera, and he began to send huge baskets of flowers to her at home. 'I don't believe it,' she'd say. 'Are you really jealous of him? You're busy all day, and I have fun with him, that's all. He's just a sweet little boy for me, nothing more.' A sweet little boy! She was only twenty herself. . . . It wasn't easy to forget her, all the time we spent in Ekaterinodar."

When the bill came, she looked it over carefully and refused to let him leave more than 10 percent for the waiter—and somehow this made it seem even stranger for them to say good night and separate in half an hour.

"Let's go to my apartment," he said sadly. "We can sit and talk a little more."

"Yes, let's go." She took his hand as she got up and drew it close to her.

A Russian cabby drove them down a deserted little side street to his apartment building. The rain looked hard as it fell through the metallic light of a gas lamp and pelted a garbage bin near the entrance. They entered the bright vestibule and took the elevator to his floor, kissing quietly as they rose in the narrow, slow-moving compartment. He had just enough time to unlock his door before the corridor light clicked off. She followed him through the apartment foyer to a little dining room, where just one bulb burned dully in a chandelier. They both looked tired; he offered her a glass of wine.

"No darling," she said. "I can't drink anymore."

He began to press. "Just one glass of white wine. I have a nice bottle of Pouilly chilling on the windowsill."

"You go ahead, love. I'm going to wash and get undressed. And sleep—sleep. You and I aren't children. I'm sure you knew that when I agreed to come here with you. . . . And really, why should we be apart?"

Too flustered to answer, he led her silently through the bedroom and turned on the lights in the bathroom. It was warm there from the furnace, and the lamps burned brightly while the rain continued drumming on the roof. She began to pull her dress over her head without closing the door.

He left and quickly drank two glasses of icy, bitter wine— and still unable to calm himself, went back into the bedroom. A mirror hung on the wall opposite the bathroom door, and he could see her there—could see all her strong, light-skinned body as she stood with her back to him and leaned over the sink to wash her neck and breasts.

"You can't come in!"—she threw on his dressing gown and left it hanging loose, walked toward him with her glistening breasts, her white hips and her taut, white stomach exposed. As if she were his wife, she embraced him. As if she were his wife, he embraced her—touched her cool skin, kissed her damp and lightly scented breasts, kissed the mouth and eyes from which she'd rinsed her makeup. . . .

Two days later she left her job and moved into his apartment.

In the winter he convinced her to put all of his earnings into a safe-deposit box in her name at the Bank Lyonnais. "It can't hurt us to be careful," he said. *"L'amour fait danser les ânes*—and I feel like I'm twenty—but anything could happen. . . ."

Three days after Easter he died on the subway—while reading a newspaper he suddenly tossed his head back against the seat, rolled his eyes. . . .

It was a lovely spring afternoon when she walked home from the graveyard in her mourning clothes. Soft clouds were drifting over Paris, and everything spoke of a life that was young and eternal—spoke of her life, which was finished.

At home she started cleaning the apartment. An old, grey officer's coat with a red lining was hanging in a closet in the corridor—for years he'd worn it in warm weather. She took it from the rack and pressed it to her face. She sat down on the floor, still clutching the coat, shuddering with sobs, begging someone for mercy.

[1940]

The Eve

RIDING through town to the train station: the cabby drives with terrible zeal, and we tear downhill, onto the bridge over the river. On the sandbar below, a vagrant stands with his back to the traffic, hurriedly eating some kind of filling from a dirty rag like a dog, his shoulders hunched as if braced against an oncoming blow. Draft carts rumble close behind the cab: as if trying to catch us, they shudder and roar, fly down the road, *mouzhiks* dangling their terrible boots from the sides. And all the *mouzhiks* riding there are giants: hatless and red-haired, covered in flour dust from the milling, their long red shirts hanging loose.

And then the train—a second-class compartment where some rotund gentleman in his forties sits across from me, his hair cropped short, gold-rimmed glasses on his flat nose, his nostrils flared and impudent. Too superior to look at me, he gets up constantly to adjust his luggage in the rack—good cases with hard exteriors. A neat and well-kept gentleman, he's relaxed and easy with his privilege, his daunting arrogance.

But already it was passing, the fall of 1916.

[1930]

Late Hour

So LONG since I was there, so long, I told myself. Not since my nineteenth year. I lived in Russia once, called it my own, had the full freedom to go where I wanted. And traveling was no great labor; I could have gone three hundred *versts* quite easily. But always I delayed. The years moved on, decades passed, and now there's no more time for waiting. Go now, or never go. This is the last and final chance, for the hour is late, and no one will meet me.

So I crossed the bridge over the river, seeing far into the distance in the July moonlight.

The bridge was so familiar that I felt I'd seen it only yesterday: humpbacked and crudely aged, as if instead of being built with stone, it was formed from something else that slowly petrified, turned hard and indestructible with time. As a boy, I used to think it was already bending over the water when Batu reigned. But in this town the bridge and the ruined walls on the cliff below the cathedral are all that speak of ancient days. The rest is simply old, provincial. It was only when I looked down that something struck me as strange, and I realized that the world had changed since I was a boy: earlier you couldn't sail the river. But now, apparently, they'd deepened it and cleared the rocks and snags. The moon was to my left, quite high above the river. In its unsteady light and the trembling sheen of the water, I could see a white paddle-wheel steamer with all its lamps burning: the portals glowed like unmoving, golden eyes, and the lights' reflections formed long columns as they stretched across the water: the ship stood silently on them, as if abandoned. I've seen the same on the Suez Canal, in Yaroslavl, and on the Nile. But in Paris the nights are thick and damp. A pinkish haze spreads across the impenetrable sky, the Seine flows black as tar beneath the bridges, and all the big columns of light falling from their lamps turn into tricolors on the water's surface: white, blue, and red—the colors of the Russian flag. Here there are no lamps, and the bridge is dry and dusty. A fire tower rises over the town and the black gardens on the hill ahead. My God, what happiness it was! During the night of the wildfire I kissed your hand for the first time, and you squeezed my fingers in response. I will never forget that secret gesture of consent. In the eerie light of the flames, all the street was black with crowds. I'd been at your house when the alarm bell rang, and everyone rushed to the windows, then hurried to the gate. The fire was far beyond the river, but it burned with terrifying greed and urgency. Smoke poured into thick clouds of blackened, purple fleece, and the flames billowed in the air like huge red sails of calico, their reflections forming copper waves in the nearby dome of Michael the Archangel's

Church. In the confusion of a frightened crowd, pressed by simple people speaking with concern, excitement, and alarm, I smelled your hair, your neck, your gingham dress, and suddenly, everything was clear: trembling, I took your hand. . . .

I climbed the hill beyond the bridge, walked the pavement into town.

There was no one there, and not one light was burning in the houses. The wide, mute streets were full of that peaceful sadness that comes to every Russian town sleeping in the steppe. Only the gardens could be heard—a cautious rustling of leaves in a weak and even wind that began somewhere in the fields, trailed through town, passed softly over me. I walked, and the big moon followed like a brilliant disk rocking its way through the black branches. Shade covered most of the streets, but houses on the right stood out sharp and clear with their white walls in the moonlight, a black luster spilling from their darkened windowpanes. I stepped on shadows that lay like black silk lace across the dappled pavement. She had a long and narrow evening dress of lace. It was fitted to her waist; it matched her young, black eyes. When she wore it she was so mysterious, so unaware of me, that I was hurt. Whose house were we visiting? Where were we when she wore that dress?

I'd planned to visit Old Street, and I could have gone there by another, shorter route. But instead I followed the wide streets through the gardens and went to see my school. I was surprised again when I reached it. Everything had stayed the same for half a century: a stone wall and a stone courtyard, a big stone building in the center of it all—everything as colorless and dull as it had been when I was there. I lingered by the gate and tried to feel the self-indulgent sadness of remembrance, and couldn't. Yes, a first-grade boy with his hair cropped short walked through this gate.

He wore a blue cadet's cap with little silver palms above the brim, a new overcoat with polished buttons. And then he turned into a thin young man wearing a grey jacket and stylish pants with stirrups: again and again he crossed this yard. But was that me?

Old Street seemed only to have narrowed. Nothing else had changed: dusty merchant houses still lined both its sides, there were still no trees, and the road was still full of potholes. The sidewalk was riddled with holes as well, so I kept to the middle of the street, where I could see my feet in the moonlight. . . . And the night was like another night—that one at the end of August, when I wore a long shirt and a narrow belt, and apples lay in mounds in the markets, and we could smell them everywhere in the warm, dark air. Are you able to remember such a night in the place that you inhabit now?

I couldn't bring myself to visit your old house. It too was probably the same—but that would make it all the more unbearable to see. I couldn't look at those unchanged rooms, where new, strange people live. Your mother and your father, your brother—they all outlived you, but they died in turn. And many others close to me have died—not only relatives but friends and mere acquaintances who started life with me. How long ago we all began to live. They were sure there would be no end: but it all began, it all flowed on, passed before my eyes—so quickly before my eyes! Sitting on a curbstone before the tall, locked gate of some merchant house, I imagined her in that distant time when we were together: her dark hair tied back, her clear eyes and her youthful, suntanned face; the strength and purity, the freedom of a young body under a light summer dress. That was the start of our love, our closeness, and our joy. A time when happiness was

clouded by nothing, when trust was transparent and tenderness a kind of ecstasy.

There's something in the warm, light nights of provincial Russian towns at the end of summer—a kind of peace, a certainty that you are safe. An old night watchman with a *kolotushka* wanders around the dark town, but only for his own pleasure: there's nothing to guard. Sleep well, good people—like providence, this boundless, glowing night is watching over you. And the old man who rattles his *kolotushka* to amuse himself as he walks on roads still warm from the day—he looks at the sky without a care. On a night like that, at that late hour when only he was awake, you waited for me among the dry leaves of late summer. I slipped through the gate you'd unlocked, quietly ran through the courtyard. And on the other side of the barn, at the far edge of that courtyard, I entered the mottled twilight of the garden, where faintly I could see your white dress in the distance: you were sitting on a bench under an apple tree. I hurried there, and when you raised your hopeful, shining eyes to me, I was filled with joy and fear.

We sat stupefied with happiness. I put my arm around you and could hear your beating heart; I held your hand and all of you was there. It grew so late that even the *kolotushka* fell silent—the old man had lain down on a bench somewhere and dozed off, warming himself in the moonlight, a pipe still clamped between his teeth. When I looked to my right, I saw the moon hanging high and pure above the courtyard, the house's roof shining like fish scales in its light. When I looked to my left, I saw a little path overgrown with dry weeds that trailed off into an apple orchard, and from behind the orchard trees I glimpsed a single green star. Suspended somewhere over another garden, it burned calmly but expectantly; it was saying something without words. But I looked only briefly at the courtyard and that star: all that mattered in the world was the twilight and your glistening eyes.

You walked me from the garden, and I said: "If there is a future life, and we meet in it, I will kneel down and kiss your feet for everything you've given me on earth." Then I stepped into the middle of the moonlit road and started walking to my house. And when I turned, I saw a whiteness still at your gate.

I got up from the curbstone and started down the road the way I'd come. Old Street wasn't all I'd planned to see. I had another aim in mind—one I'd hidden from myself while knowing all along it was inevitable. And so I started out in that direction—I would visit one more place, and leave for good.

Once again, I knew the way: straight ahead, straight ahead, then left at the bazaar, and out from town on Monastery Road.

The bazaar is like another town within the town. Each row has its own distinctive smell. Awnings cast a gloom over the long tables and benches where people eat. In the middle of the hardware aisle, an icon hangs on a chain: the Savior stares with his eyes wide open from a rusty frame. In the morning fat pigeons flock around the bakers' stalls, run and peck at crumbs. You walk to school and you're amazed, somehow, by all these pigeons—how rainbows shine around their necks, how they bob their heads in rhythm, rock from side to side, mince as if they're trying to be coquettes. They act as if you don't exist until the last possible moment, then burst into flight from under your feet, rise on their whistling wings. At night, big rats come out and scurry through the stalls, intent on something, terrifying, dark and foul.

Monastery Road's a quick and easy route into the fields. Some travel it to their houses in the countryside; others to the city of the dead. In Paris the entrance to some nondescript house will suddenly take on the trappings of a play about the plague, and for two days these morbid decorations will set the house apart from all the others on its street. The front door is draped in black and silver crepe, and a piece of paper edged in black is set neatly on a table under a black cloth in the entranceway. For forty-eight hours polite visitors write their names here as a sign of sympathy, and then, at some last, appointed hour, a huge hearse with a black canopy rolls up. The rounded edges of the canopy are decorated with big white stars in order to preserve our dreams of heaven, but the wooden carriage frame itself is pitch black, like a plague coffin, and black plumes flutter from the corners of the roof like ostrich feathers from the underworld. The massive creatures pulling it are draped in coal-black studded cloths with little eyelets rimmed in white. Waiting for the body to be carried out, an old drunk sits on the towering driver's box. He too must be attired for the occasion, so he wears a somber tricorn and a mourning coat to play his role, even though he's prone to smirking at those solemn words: *Requiem aeternam dona eis, Domine, et lux perpetua luceat eis.* . . . Here it's all done differently. An open coffin's carried on linen cloths into the breeze that blows down Monastery Road. A rice-white face rocks from side to side with its heavy eyelids shut, a bright paper band around the forehead. This is how they carried her away.

Built in the time of Tsar Aleksey Mikhaylovich, the monastery stands like a fortress at the edge of town, just left of the highway. Its gates are always locked, and forbidding walls surround the cathedral's golden domes. But farther on, already in the open countryside, low walls enclose a wide grove of birches, elms, and limes. Long, intersecting avenues run through the grove; monuments and crosses are spread among the trees beside them.

There the gate was open wide, and I could see the main avenue—smooth and endless. Timidly I took off my hat and went into the grove. Such a late and silent hour! The moon was hanging low behind the trees, but everything was clear: I could see the full expanse of that forest of the dead, the pattern of its monuments and crosses in the limpid shade. The wind had settled; patches of darkness and light that had trembled under the trees now lay motionless in the hour before dawn. Suddenly something stirred at the far end of the grove. From behind the graveyard church it flashed with terrible speed, flew at me like a black ball: outside myself, I jumped aside, my head turning to ice and tightening, my heart lurching, going still. . . . What was it? It raced away and disappeared. But my heart stayed motionless. And so, carrying my heart like a heavy cup inside my chest, I walked straight on, knowing where I had to go. At the end of the path I came to a patch of level ground that was overgrown with dry grass. There an isolated, narrow slab of stone lay facing out from the back wall of the cemetery. And from behind the wall, a green star hung like a brilliant gem. It glowed like that earlier star, but it was mute and still.

[1938]

Notes

Sunstroke

botvinya: A cold soup of fish, herbs, and *kvass*, a dark, fermented drink made from rye or barley.

Raven

Niva: A popular illustrated journal, published in Saint Petersburg from 1870 to 1918.

Patronymic: Referring to someone by first name and patronymic is a sign of respect and deference. One's patronymic is formed from the first name of one's father—Yelena's father is Nikolay; her patronymic consists of a feminine ending, *evna*, attached to this name.

Patience: A card game similar to solitaire.

Ida

Bolshoy Moskovsky: A well-known Moscow restaurant. Literally "The Big Moscow Restaurant."

"Do you remember the magic tablecloth from all those fairy tales you read as a child?": The composer asks the waiter to cover their table with a *samobranaya* tablecloth, which appears in many popular folk tales and magically creates food for the prince who possesses it.

ukha: Fish soup.

"Je veux un trésor qui les contient tous, je veux la jeunesse": "I want to possess that treasure that contains within it everything, I want youth."

pirog: A small turnover, often with a filling of cabbage, potatoes, or meat.

verst: Russian measurement of distance equal to 3,500 feet.

"Laissez-moi, laissez-moi contempler ton visage!": "Let me, let me look at your face."

blinis: Russian pancakes, similar to crepes.

Cranes

mouzhik: A male peasant.

Caucasus

Gelendzhik and Gagry: Cities located on the coast of the Black Sea.

Narzan: A brand of mineral water, still popular today in Russia.

dukhan: A shop or a small inn with an inexpensive restaurant, in the Caucasus and the Middle East.

Ballad

. . . every room glowed with the flames of lamps and wax candles that stood before the icons in the holy corners: Traditionally, each room in a Russian house would have a *krasny ugol*, literally a "beautiful corner," where an icon was hung.

"It all took place during the reign of the Great Tsarina": Catherine the Great.

Cold Fall

"*Such a cold fall!*": From a poem by A. A. Fet (1820–1892), one of Bunin's favorite writers.

The Gentleman from San Francisco

tarantella: A fast, whirling dance performed in southern Italy.

tramontana: A cold northern wind that blows in the western Mediterranean.

Ischia and Capri: Islands just off the Italian coast.

"*Na sonata, Signore?*": "You called, Sir?"

"*Gia e morto*": "He is already dead."

"*Pronto?*": "Ready?"

"Partenza!": "Departure!"

Two thousand years ago that island was inhabited by a man who some-how held power over millions of people: Tiberius Claudius Nero Cae-sar, emperor of Rome from 14 B.C. to A.D. 37.

Muza

Muza: The names in this story have obvious connotations for a Russian reader. Muza is literally "Muse." Zavistovsky's name comes from the Russian word for envy, *zavist.*

Prague Restaurant: A very fashionable and expensive Moscow restau-rant.

fortochka: A small, hinged pane of glass set inside a window, which can be opened for ventilation in winter.

"I saw you at Shor's concert": David Solomonovich Shor (1867–1942), a pianist and professor at the Moscow Conservatory whom Bunin knew personally.

"I was just sitting here in the twilight, enjoying a night without lamps": In Russian a single verb describes this process: *sumernichat.*

Rusya

sarafan: A peasant dress without sleeves, buttoning in front.

vareniki: A kind of dumpling made with fruit or curds.

okroshka: A cold soup made with chopped vegetables, meat, and *kvass.*

"It's no wonder the devil took the form of a snake": The Russian word for grass snake is *uzh*; the Russian word for horror is *uzhas.* Rusya actually says, "It's no wonder the word for 'horror' comes from the word for 'grass snake'" —a statement that cannot be rendered in English for obvious reasons.

Marya Viktorovna: Rusya's formal name and patronymic.

"Amata nobis quantum amabitur nulla!": "Beloved by us as no other shall be."

Styopa

Kislovodsk: A city in southern Russia, not far from the Georgian border.

Maly Theatre: One of Moscow's best-known drama theatres.

On One Familiar Street

"I remember one familiar street . . .": Bunin quotes loosely from "The Hermit" by Ya. P. Polonsky (1819–1889).

Serpukhov: A city roughly fifty miles southeast of Moscow.

Antigone

Averchenko: Arkady Timofeyevich Averchenko, Russian writer and humorist, 1881–1925.

"This is my Antigone," the general joked. "Although I am not as blind as Oedipus . . .": Antigone is the daughter of Oedipus; she follows her father into exile from Thebes.

When he rode into the courtyard, a line from *Onegin* had been running through his head—*My uncle is a man of utmost principles . . .*: In

A. S. Pushkin's famous work, *Evgeny Onegin*, the protagonist complains about the tedium of waiting for his uncle to die and leave him his inheritance. "My uncle is a man of utmost principles" is a rough translation of the first line of the poem's first chapter.

The current war against Japan: Fought from 1904 to 1905, the war was an embarrassing defeat for Russia.

Zoyka and Valeriya

The Kazan railway line: A Russian reader familiar with Moscow would recognize this as a sign of prosperity. The Kazan line runs south from the city to pleasant countryside with a temperate summer climate—a prime spot for dachas.

Still recovering from typhus, she wore a little cap of black silk as she half sat and half lay in an armchair nearby: It was common practice to shave the heads of people suffering from typhus in order to combat the lice that carry the disease.

"May we call you Valechka?" A diminutive, affectionate form of Valeriya.

"The dark woods smell of pitch and wild berries. . . ." From A. K. Tolstoy's "Ilya Muromets."

Why did she call him "thou" one day and "you" the next? In Russian there are two forms of the word "you": the formal *vy*, and the informal *ty*. Addressing someone as *ty* would imply greater intimacy than the *vy* form.

tvorog: A kind of curd.

Valya: The short, familiar variant of Valeriya.

In Paris

"Rien n'est plus difficile que de reconnaître un bon melon et une femme de bien": "Nothing is more difficult than judging by sight the ripeness of a watermelon and the virtue of a woman."

zubrovka: Sweetgrass vodka.

"L'eau gâte le vin comme la charrette le chemin et la femme—l'âme": "Water ruins wine the way a cart ruins the road, and a woman—the soul."

"Caviar rouge, salad russe. . . . Deaux shashliks. . . .": "Red caviar, Russian salad. . . . Two shashliks."

The Great War: World War I.

"C'est moi qui vous remercie": "It is I who am grateful to you."

"Le bon Dieu envoie toujours des culottes à ceux qui n'ont pas de derrière. . . .": "Merciful God always gives pants to those who lack rear ends."

"Qui se marie par amour a bonnes nuits et mauvais jours": "He who marries for love has good nights and bad days."

"Patience—médecine des pauvres": "Patience is the medicine of the poor."

"L'amour fait danser les ânes": "Love makes even donkeys dance."

Late Hour

kolotushka: A kind of large wooden clapper or rattle used as an alarm.

Requiem aeternam dona eis, Domine, et lux perpetua luceat eis: Give them eternal peace, Lord, and let the eternal light shine for them.